THE BROTHER AND I

Formerly
From a Morning Prayer

by

John Mathias Haffert

PREFACE BY
WILLIAM A. DONAGHY, S. J.

Printed in U.S.A.
by

Ave Maria Institute
Washington, New Jersey

Nihil Obstat
JOHN M. A. FEARNS, S. T. D.
Censor Librorum

Imprimatur
✠ FRANCIS CARDINAL J. SPELLMAN, S. T. D.
Archbishop of New York

NOTE: This book is a reprint. The *Imprimatur* above was given to the chapters up to the last three which have been added to this edition with ecclesiastical permission.

CONTENTS

Msgr. Colgan
gives his
blessing to
Blue Army
leaders at
Seminar in
New York.

FOR ALMOST four centuries now the heresy of man's self-sufficiency has brought woe upon the human race. The emergence of the human Ego, the shift of focus from God to man as the center of the universe, brought chaos into theology, philosophy, economics and the whole concept of society.

In theology, man was his own interpreter and needed no infallible Church; in philosophy, he bounded his mind by the limits of material objects and either denied or depreciated the spiritual; in economics, man denied that he was his brother's keeper and embarked on a devil-take-the-hindmost kind of commerce which brought the poor to the wall, and created a false, mercantile aristocracy. Man came to think that he was quite able to take care of himself, that he was hard-headed, practical, conqueror of the mysteries of nature through science.

Now, however, human nature is not so sure of itself. Now that the sad bugle-melody of "Taps" has become the national anthem of nations once proud and mighty, the myth of man's self-sufficiency lies shattered. More and more we are coming to realize that man without God is a savage, that civilization without God is a sham which, by the slow working of natural causes, must inevitably become a shambles. Many of us, as Edmund Burke said, would have no teacher but experience. Twice in the lifetime of adults has experience demonstrated these truths in two great wars.

Confused and bewildered, with what they had considered as an unshakable set of values broken into shards, men need now a new certitude, a new hope. When he was happy, when the wine flowed and the dance was loud and error walked attractively garbed, the preaching of the Church fell hollowly on man's ear. But now that he is down in the primordial mud fighting for his life, and error has thrown aside the lamp of pseudo-knowledge to pick up instead a flame-thrower, man is turning in desperation to God. He is ready for a spiritual rebirth, a reunion with the Father Whom he deserted long ago. He has lived riotously, his coinage is gone, his soul revolted by husks; he is ready to return.

The role of the Blessed Mother in such a rebirth is obvious. She was the Mother of God; He, in His last bloody testament, made her likewise the Mother of Men; through her the world could be spiritually regenerated. As St. Augustine says: "She is the Mother of His members because by her love she co-operated that the faithful members of that Head might be born in the Church." Pope Pius X points out the same lovely concept and openly declares "She administers the treasury of Christ's merits with

full maternal right." The power of her intercession
and her motherly influence with her Divine Son is
described strikingly in the words of Leo XIII: "The
only begotten Son of God in no doubtful manner
showed His reverence for His Most Holy Mother.
While still living His hidden life He made her an
associate in the ministry of both wonders He
wrought: the one of grace, when upon the saluta-
tion of Mary the infant leaped in the womb of Eliza-
beth; the other of nature, when He changed water
into wine at the wedding of Cana." She is no less
aware of our needs now than she was conscious of
the embarrassing development at that little country
wedding centuries ago. Her influence and interces-
sory power are no less great.

Hence, the timeliness of Mr. Haffert's solidly pious
book, *"From a Morning Prayer,"* is patent. It is
a call to turn back to Mary, to walk that ancient
path to which the Fathers so often directed us: *To
Jesus through Mary.* She is, in another metaphor
frequently used by the Fathers, the "bridge" where-
by we can go back to God. She is "our life, our
sweetness and our hope."

May she gather all of us unto Him Who is the
way, the truth, the life. May she call back those
who have lost the way and who blunder along de-
tours of sin. Many are hostile to her and scoff at
her. To them we address the glowingly Christian
words of Cardinal Newman: "May that bright and

gentle Lady, the Blessed Virgin Mary, overcome you with her sweetness, and revenge herself on her foes by interceding effectually for their conversion."

WILLIAM A. DONAGHY, S. J.

July 16th, 1943

A climax to the apostolate described in this book came on May 13th, 1971, when Bishops simultaneously crowned statues of Our Lady of Fatima for seventy nations around the entire world.

AUTHOR'S FOREWORD

SOMEONE SAID of this book, without intending that I should hear, that it was "dynamite."

By that he meant that the book is spiritually frank, almost to the danger point; that it is "ticklish" in the sense that one hardly knows how, in the hands of a wide variety of readers, it will explode.

But sometimes dynamite is necessary. Obstacles that would take years to remove by hand labor can frequently be removed by one charge of dynamite.

The obstacle to be overcome by these pages is inertia. And one could give countless examples of the obstinacy of inertia as a power to prevent the growth of a religious idea . . . not only of *any* religious idea but of the very one to which this book applies a little "dynamite." That is why it has been written.

For five years, I wondered how I might write this book without using any proper names, and without revealing myself. Finally, it was not only because I could find no solution to this problem that I gave in to it. It was also because I saw the senselessness of worrying about such worthless things as names. The two facts . . . that the characters of the book are living and that the writer is the most continually appearing figure in most of the narration . . . neither add to nor much detract from *the mes-*

sage in the book. And that message, however poorly written, may just as well start on its way now as
twenty years from now . . . when a generation of
Catholics will have missed it.

The greatest harm that could come from this dynamite . . . if, indeed, any harm could come of it
. . . is to myself. For many will undoubtedly accuse
me of show, and some may do me the even greater
injustice of thinking me saintly.

But I do not think that anyone will read this story
and not be convinced. For I was myself convinced
to the point of great sacrifice, and every skeptic this
story has met thus far has become its apostle.

That everyone may receive it in the spirit in which
it is written is my earnest and heartfelt prayer. For
thus received, it will be a dynamite that may blast
a wonderful message into its readers' hearts.

I well remember that Monsignor Fulton Sheen
said to me: "You are doing a wonderful work."
And when I answered that the degree of goodness
in my work was certainly not the slightest ray in
comparison to the good he was accomplishing, he
made an answer I shall never forget:

"It is a case," he said, "of opportunity."

By that he meant "of a following."

To have a personal following is important to a
leader in any field. People like to deal personally
with an acknowledged leader. They appreciate the
autographed book, the signed letter, the hand-shake.

This contact is as though they had entered into the heart of the ideal or of the organization they are following, and they themselves more readily become apostles.

To be a leader in a Scapular apostolate was not of my choosing. Indeed, it would have been far easier for me at many points along the road to make a choice more to my personal liking. But since leadership has fallen to me as a trust, I shall use the abovementioned psychology to its utmost. And in that fact one has the explanation of much of the outrightness in this book.

May God bless those who have made it possible! And may the reading of these pages be a source of increased admiration and love of His Mother, in whose honor they were written.

J. M. H.

In 1971: John Haffert, U. S. leader of the Blue Army, with Rev. Georges M. Domanski, successor of Blessed Maximilian Kolbe as Father Guardian of MARYTOWN, near Warsaw, in Poland. The picture was taken on May 15th, as Mr. Haffert was returning from the coronation of the Pilgrim Virgin in Moscow. This chapel at Marytown had been completely redecorated for the coronation (which took place simultaneously around the world on last May 13th). The National Pilgrim of Poland is seen over the altar. Father Domanski said: "It seems to me that he (Bl. Maximilian) is the Patron of all Marian Armies to conquer as soon as possible, all the world to Christ through the Immaculate."

"E fructibus eorum cognosce eos."

Matt.—xii, 33

CHAPTER TWO

The First Meeting

WHAT YOU are about to read is true, unusual though some of the things I have to tell may prove to be.

Some years ago, in a great, grey-stone seminary of the Carmelites, I made my simple profession of Poverty, Chastity, and Obedience to the Carmelite Rule. As I lay on the tile floor, prostrate before the Blessed Sacrament, oblivious to the crowded chapel, with tears of joy streaming down my cheeks as the glorious tones of the *Te Deum* rose from the choir and echoed from the rafters, I little thought that three years later I would be shedding tears of heart-break in a Pullman berth . . . leaving that monastery, after having striven to become a Carmelite priest for eight years.

But I could not go on to solemn vows.

And when, after so long an absence, I returned home to parents who had idolized me and idealized me, I was highly sensitive, with a dozen battles going on at once within me.

A short time later, I received a position as teacher of French in another Carmelite seminary (at

1

Middletown, New York) and had little time to worry about myself and my future.

That new-found vocation was probably the first thing that began to shock my skepticism about the extraordinary things I want to tell you . . . all in due time.

MY STORY could begin in many places; taken chronologically it would not make very interesting reading nor great sense. I think it will make the most sense if I begin right at the time the extraordinary things began to happen. That was when I was a Carmelite novice, at a general recreation on New Year's day.

A "general recreation" is one in which Novices, who are otherwise entirely segregated, may speak to everyone in the Community.

I had looked forward to this recreation with particular anticipation. I was anxious to speak with a little lay-brother whom, during my four years as a postulant, I had always considered saintly. Now my curiosity was edged regarding him particularly because my best friend (who was my room-mate in the Novitiate and who had progressed so far on the way to sanctity before he took the Habit that I looked to him for counsel and advice in everything) customarily spoke of this brother in awed tones.

As the members of the Community began to file into the Novitiate recreation room, my friend and I stood by the door waiting for the lay-brother (to whom, in this book, we will refer simply as "Brother," or "the lay-brother").

Of course it was my friend who really knew Brother. I had merely admired him from a distance. Not long after I first became a postulant I learned that this Brother had started out to become a priest, but that he went almost blind. Rather than give up his vocation altogether, he then received permission to become a lay-brother, and within two days his sight was completely restored. When he wanted to become a priest again, his advisor counselled him to accept what had happened so inexplicably as a sign, and to remain a brother. Moreover, I also knew, on good authority, that with hardly any higher education, this Brother had such an extensive knowledge of theology, both dogmatic and moral, that sometimes priests sought counsel from him. (I later witnessed this fact myself.)

When Brother finally arrived, my friend seized his arm and at once engaged in a spritely conversation about family, books, news.

He was a small man . . . this quiet little brother . . . with thinning, black hair, luminous, dark eyes, and a round, jolly face that seemed out of proportion to his slight body. He had little to say in the conversation, but somehow seemed to be wholeheartedly participating.

A short time later, my friend was called away and I suddenly found myself alone with the Brother, talking to him as though I had known him all my life. I was remarking on the joy I found in being a religious. Suddenly, with no preface, he said:

"How do you feel about your vocation, now?"

The "Now" had such an explosive connotation that my jaw fell open.

"I have never been so happy, Brother," I said, recovering myself. "I love religious life."

"I'm glad," Brother said. 'When you were faltering in your vocation last year I went to Father John (his advisor and, by coincidence, also my own . . . from earliest childhood) and told him to watch over you. I prayed earnestly for you."

"But," I exclaimed, no longer trying to hide my now confirmed amazement, "how did you know that I ever faltered in my vocation? I have not even known you, and that is a secret I have never shared with even my best friend."

Brother smiled, probably at the expression on my face. "I passed you one day in the corridor and it was written plainly on your face."

I was silent.

I did not suspect anything preternatural. But how could anything of this kind have been "written on my face"? Brother was right in his conviction that I had faltered in my vocation. But I had not gone through any inward struggle over my vocation while I was in the seminary. The faltering had come about during a summer vacation, at the time Brother mentioned, over a girl I had met at a beach-party. She was a pretty girl, dark, attractive, not very spiritual, and had so captivated me that I became utterly rash in my devotion for her. And I cannot say yet what changed me. But I did go back to the seminary and, once out of her bewitching company, I got down to my books and wondered how I could have been so foolish. But not even my closest friend . . . with whom I spent most of my waking hours because proximity in seniority placed us together at the table, in the chapel, in the dormitory, everywhere . . . will know that I faltered in my vocation until he reads these lines!

Then Brother began to talk to me about the Blessed Virgin. He certainly touched the warmest spot in my heart, because I had been avidly reading everything about Her that I could get my hands upon. The conversation became intense and I found myself betraying a fact that I had just learned in the Novitiate, but which seemed to be all that was beautiful and good in life: *Union with Our Lady.*

"I think that union with Her, Brother," I said with the air of one imparting a great finding, "is the secret of quick and secure sanctity, because if

God sees Mary in us, He will unite Himself to us and give Himself to us entirely. I think it is quick, because it would take a life-time to obtain an immaculate spirit, and it takes only a heartfelt wish to unite us morally to the Immaculate. And I think it is secure because Mary, a real Mother, guides us and protects us in the ways of virtue, and even imparts to us Her own virtues."

Brother listened attentively, with obvious satisfaction . . . amazingly as though he were a teacher, proud of a student's well-recited lesson.

When the recreation was over, I pondered my surprise. And I felt a little ashamed of my loquacity, over a new-found sanctity, with a man who had probably lived that message for years and had reached heights known only to God Himself.

But that strange conversation was the beginning of a stranger drama . . . a drama that was, as we shall see, to affect millions of Catholics.

"Brother"

During the twenty years since this book was first published the "Brother" was unknown. But in 1954, with permission of the Carmelite Fathers, he accepted the invitation
of the Most Reverend Charles P. Greco, D.D., Bishop of
Alexandria, La., to found a new congregation of Brothers
for diocesan secretarial, teaching, and social work. The
Brother is shown here in the habit of the new Community,
the Brothers of the Holy Eucharist. In 1961 the Community
had five houses, with motherhouse in Bunkie, La. In June
of this year, John Haffert and the Brother were united for
the first time in seven years on the occasion of Father John's
50th anniversary of ordination, celebrated at the Philadelphia Carmel where Haffert's sister (Sr. Therese of the Queen
of Carmel) was completing her twentieth year.

At the world centre of the Blue Army in Fatima
representatives from many nations carry their
flags to accompany the Icon of Our Lady of Kazan, Patroness of Russia, to the Blue Army By-
zantine Chapel to await restoration to the people
of Russia.

CHAPTER THREE

Who Is He?

THE MOST important person in this drama, as the reader can probably gather, will prove to be this lay-brother. He will appear in these pages, and then suddenly bow out after having left the negative of a wonderful message, to be developed, and duplicated millions of times.

It is about twenty years since the day Brother applied for admission to study for the Carmelite priesthood. He was an American of Sicilian extraction. His father owned a butcher shop in a Mid-Western city. His mother, who could not speak English, was a pious woman who had tried repeatedly to join a cloistered community in Sicily. She was finally accepted . . . but was later forced to return to the world because her health failed. Although greatly crushed, she knew how to say: "Thy Will be done!" She married, and came to America with her husband. She raised a family of seven, among whom Brother was her favorite.

When he was five years old, as Brother confided to me in later years, his mother found him lying on his bed, stretching his arms upwards and sobbing through copious tears: "I want to die and go to Heaven! I want to die and go to Heaven!"

But this was not all that led Brother's mother to hope particularly in him. Once, after she had prayed with unusual fervor to Saint Therese of Lisieux for her seven children, she walked into her living room and found seven fresh roses lying beneath a picture of St. Therese. Six were red and one was white. "The white one," she thought, "is . . ." and she mentioned Brother's name.

I have had the privilege of meeting Brother's mother and of studying her as a skeptic would study the syllogism of a conclusion that seems fabulous. And, in her dark, swimming eyes, I saw a great deal of common sense and fathoms of purity and of divine love. I somehow knew that being close to her I was not far from the Divinity. I had no doubt that even extraordinary favors were not unusual with her.

Little though I may evidence the fact, in the following pages, I am really quite skeptical about extraordinary favors, unless they have happened in the past and have some corroboration . . . like the miracles of Lourdes confirming the vision of Bernadette, miracles confirming the Scapular vision, and the like. It was a long while before I said a *full* "Credo" to the extraordinary happening that is the focal point of this book, and it was only my belief in *that* that really settled my skepticism about many other things of which I shall speak.

However, to get back to Brother's entry into Carmel:

The Master of Novices at that time was Father John, whom we have already mentioned.

During the winter, shortly after Brother . . . then hardly more than a boy . . . had become a Novice, Father John noticed one day that there were no blankets in his room. He immediately asked:

"Where are your blankets?"

The Novice-brother looked frightened.

"I . . . I'm not very cold, Father," he said. "I don't need blankets very much."

Trying to hide his amazement at such extreme mortification, Father John murmured something about pneumonia and told Brother to get blankets at once, because the nights were bitter-cold.

It was not long after this that Brother had his first experience of what seemed to be a vision.

It is almost sacrilegious to put the fact of this favor so bluntly. It was cajoled from Brother, twelve years later, with the gravest difficulty, with multiple arguments and an air of great sacredness, and only then did I learn it falteringly and with his long preface about the little faith we should put in extraordinary favors. And, above all, had I the pen of Werfel I could not describe the look in his eyes as he recreated what he had seen.

"One night, not knowing whether I was awake or dreaming," Brother said, "I saw a very beautiful lady writing in an immense book. The letters, as she inscribed them, shone like real gold, gleaming in the brilliant light that radiated from her. When she had finished, I saw that it was *my name* she had written! And then she turned and smiled at me . . . "

It was almost as though Brother were seeing his lady for the first time. I was spell-bound. His deep brown eyes were like pools reflecting some beautiful, hidden radiance.

"It was the Blessed Virgin!" I said.

To that, Brother made no answer. With an air of heavy seriousness, almost as though to share the secret were to lose it, he said: "That smile was so sweet that it impressed itself indelibly in my heart so that I need but think of it to see it again."

Although that is all that I could get from him . . . and with what persuasive arguments, the reader will see later . . . I felt sure he had not told me everything.

But I had learned enough to give myself great food for thought.

Who was this wonderful little man whose life was to wind through mine like a stream of crystal spring-water mingling with a brook . . . a brook that even yet so much likes the taste of earth that it caresses its banks lingeringly and is unashamed of its own babbling?

The Brother and I – in 1945 – just after Brother returned from ten years in Palestine.

CHAPTER FOUR

Signs

I BEGAN to make a study of this wonderful Carmelite. There were few of my fellow religious who were able to aid me. Most thought Brother extremely good, even saintly. A few thought him eccentric. No one disliked him, but neither did there seem to be anyone who could claim to be close to him.

Therefore I observed. I talked to Brother as much as I could and I took every opportunity to study him for any signs that might betray his true nature.

Before long, my main observation was that this little man, who seemed so ordinary, was practicing extraordinary virtue.

One of the best examples I can give is the strange thing I observed at an unusually interesting Provincial chapter.

The Provincial in office had served four terms, and there was a close division of opinion as to whether he or another would be elected. The vote had been cast several times, and several times it

14

had been a tie. More than personalities were at stake. And it was difficult to say which way the powers of the Province, gathered at the house for this momentous meeting, would cast their lot.

Crowding outside the chapter-room door, as was the custom when the lots were cast, all the members of the community who were not participating in the chapter waited to see the door open.

Standing in a doorway with the crowd in the corridor, I was watching Brother. He did not see me. Enjoying the extraordinary privilege of talking in the corridor on this special occasion, he was laughing and participating in a conversation that engrossed the little group chatting to him. Every once in a while, being short, he stood on tiptoe and strained towards the chapter-room door, apparently the most anxious person in the corridor to see who was going to come through the door first.

Finally, as though by some secret communication, the talking in the corridor died. All faces were turned towards the chapter-room door. The scraping of chairs revealed that the voting had been completed and that one of the two candidates had been elected.

Standing hidden in the doorway, entirely ignored in the pitch of excitement, I kept my eyes fixed on Brother. Was he, then, not at all to mortify his curiosity? There he was, stretched on tiptoe, with apparently the most natural and most expectant of all the faces I could see.

Suddenly, while one might have heard a pin drop, the knob of the chapter-room door turned noisily.

Brother, still on tiptoe, no one noticing him (except myself, of course) *had closed his eyes,* mortifying himself after a long show of curiosity!

Shortly after this chapter, the ex-Provincial died at Niagara Falls while Brother was visiting in Chicago, and Brother knew about his death before he was told about it.

Perhaps he guessed it?

Once, almost with a touch of comedy, this remarkable power did not work to the good fortune of the Novice-Brothers, over whom Brother had jurisdiction.

Brother came into the choir-loft one afternoon and, after a prayer, he sat down at the organ to work on an *Ave Maria* he was composing. (Brother painted and also played the organ; he never had training in either art, but he did manifest some native talent.) He had just seated himself and was about to begin, when his hands stopped over the keys and that far-away look came into his eyes. After a moment, his hands changed their direction and reached for the music, folded it, closed the organ, put the music away, and Brother went out.

I discovered later that he went down to the kitchen . . . which was a good distance from the chapel

. . . and caught his young protegés in the act of taking an illicit snack!

On another occasion I was talking to him, alone. He was listening to what I said and occasionally passing judgment. A great deal of time had passed, and still the subject seemed inexhaustible. Suddenly, however, I noticed that Brother was not listening to me.

"Is something wrong, Brother?" I asked.

"Would you excuse me," he asked apologetically, "but I think someone is looking for me."

"Oh, nonsense, Brother!" I exclaimed. "Whatever could give you that idea? We've been here an hour and there has been no sign of someone looking for you."

"Well," the Brother said, with a smile that made the expected permission pleasurable, "I'll only be gone a moment. Wait for me."

I cannot say what peculiar feeling crept over me . . . whether eeriness, amazement, incredulity, or curiosity, or all four together. It really seemed as though some person in the room, whom I could not see, had spoken to the Brother.

A short time later, he came back . . . and quietly resumed his seat as though nothing had happened.

"Was someone really looking for you?" I asked, with obvious awe.

"Oh . . . it wasn't anything important . . . just someone delivering produce down at the cellar door

and I have the keys. He could have left it there
. . . but then, you know the boys."

However, this is straying from my observation of
his virtues, of which humility was one of the most
salient. An example of this was afforded me many
times, and usually to my chagrin. I could never get
Brother to talk about himself. The greatest com-
mitment I was able to have him make was: "To me,
prayer is an embrace with God, and it can last for
hours."

On one particular occasion, for instance, I was
talking to him about the Blessed Virgin, and he so
forgot himself that he suddenly exclaimed: "Oh . . .
if we had only one *drop* of the love that filled the
heart of Mary as She stood beneath the Cross, we
would be lost in an ocean of love!" And he seemed
almost to go into an ecstacy. I could never, even
were I the most gifted of writers, depict the expression on his face. His eyes were luminous and
there was a wonderful quiver of emotion about his
mouth.

"My! Brother," I involuntarily exclaimed, "how
you love the Blessed Virgin!"

Instantly his face changed. He became flushed,
and was filled with confusion.

"If I do," he said hastily, "it is by the Grace of
God . . . it is by the Grace of God. Never say that."

And never again, much though I tried, could I

ever draw him to speak unreservedly about love for Mary!

Were I to use every other page in this book to talk about Brother, I do not feel that I could do justice to the wonderful purity of soul, abandonment to God's Will, and humility which I discovered in him.

The Brother and I in 1967, at the Motherhouse of the Brothers of the Holy Eucharist.

CHAPTER FIVE

A Morning Prayer

FOR EVERY conversation with Brother I had to obtain specific permission from my Master or from the Prior . . . and these superiors soon began to be worried about the frequency of the conversations. The rule was that clerics should not talk to lay-brothers, and I had a suspicion that permission would not be granted much more often.

Such was my observation to Brother on this particular November day. We had been walking on the campus. Our conversations of late had taken a very practical turn: each used the conversation of the other to draw closer to Mary (although it was a particularly "me-sided" advantage). We had just been wondering whether we were not living in an age when all men should be borrowing a little of that same practicality, and had stopped in front of the chapel before parting. Then, like a bolt of lightning, a surprising thing happened to me.

I shall never forget any detail. I remember where I stood, where Brother stood . . . under the arch at the chapel entrance . . . on a grey November day.

We had just spoken at length about the value of true devotion to Mary and what a wonder that devotion would work on all mankind were men but to practice it.

Suddenly, as though I were hypnotized, I heard words coming from my mouth that were not in my mind! It seemed unbelievable.

"Brother," the words ran, *"It is for you to find a way to lead men to Jesus through Mary without words."*

Brother saw the startled look on my face.

But I saw an even stranger expression on his.

He seemed to be hearing his life sentence. His eyes were intense, his body rigid, his brow furrowed with lines of concentration.

Without another word, we parted.

All that afternoon and evening, I felt that something was going to happen . . . to Brother or to me . . . possibly even something extraordinary. I could not (and cannot yet) cease to be amazed at the words that came from my mouth on the chapel porch. All I could think was: "I did not say those words myself!"

The next morning, Brother came to my cell and knocked on the door. This was unusual. Ordinarily I was the one who sought him. My heart started to pound.

"Frater Mathias," he addressed me by my name in religion, his features revealing nothing, "do you remember what you said to me when we parted yesterday afternoon?"

"Yes, Brother," I answered, trying to remain calm.

"This prayer suddenly came to me last night," Brother said, drawing a piece of paper from beneath his habit. "It is a morning offering for a Scapular apostolate, and I think such an apostolate is what you mean by a devotion to draw men to the Sacred Heart through Mary, without words."

Saying this, he was gone, and I was standing in my doorway, holding a slip of paper.

Here, my personal emotions are irrelevant; so I will speak little about them. But the average reader, who is an ordinary person like myself, may imagine that he was in my place . . . closing the cell door and turning in solitude to contemplate "A morning offering for a Scapular Apostolate . . . an apostolate to draw men to the Sacred Heart, through Mary, without words."

How could a *prayer* be the basis of a *wordless* devotion? What could a Scapular apostolate be? Whatever it was, would it be so valuable that it *would* draw men to union with Jesus, through Mary?

The morning offering read as follows:

> *O my God, in union with Our Lady of Mount Carmel,*
> *I offer Thee the Precious Blood of Jesus*
> *From all the altars throughout the world,*
> *Joining with It the offering of my every thought,*
> *word and action of this day.*

*I desire to gain every indulgence and merit I
    can,*
Offering them, together with myself,
To Mary Immaculate,
*Whom Thou hast appointed the dispenser of the
    merits of Thy Precious Blood, especially by
    means of this Scapular (Here kiss the Scap-
    ular you wear—500 days indulgence),*
That She may best apply them
To the interests of Thy Most Sacred Heart.
Precious Blood of Jesus, save us!
Our Lady of Mount Carmel, pray for us!
Sacred Heart of Jesus, have mercy on us!

I cannot say that I did not understand, because
I felt that, at least mistily, I did understand. But
I was somewhat confused and disappointed.

"O my God, in union with the Immaculate Heart
of Mary, I offer Thee the Precious Blood . . . and
join with It the offering of my every action," I said
to myself, trying to re-phrase the prayer to find
its secret.

But all I could find there was a repetition of the
well-known Morning Offering of the long established Apostleship of Prayer.

"I offer my actions, together with myself, to Mary
Immaculate," I continued my thoughts, "that She
may best apply them to the interests of Thy Sacred
Heart."

That was nothing more than the consecration of
Blessed Grignon de Montfort, an elaboration of
the first part of the prayer.

The only difference I could see was that, after saying, "Together with myself, to Mary Immaculate," one should kiss the Scapular.

Then my heart bounded.

Scapular Apostolate . . . wordless . . . *that was it!* The Scapular is a silent bond of *union with Mary.* Advertence to that bond would make it alive . . . alive to the point that *all we might do or think or say would be through, in union with, the Immaculate* . . . who is One with the Sacred Heart!

Thoughts came tumbling over each other.

What a glorious message! What a simple, practical aid to make the formula *"To Jesus through Mary"* more than just a formula! Here, for seven centuries, Catholics have had a bond of union with Mary . . . a bond so intimate that She Herself promised that those who cling to it cannot lose their souls! And yet, most of us seem never to have thought to use it as a *bond,* but merely as a *sign* of devotion and of predestination. How the world would be changed if all Catholics who wore the Scapular . . . some two hundred million . . . were to advert to the fact that the Scapular made them Mary's chosen ones, as the Church sings in the Preface of the Mass on the Scapular Feast. And what if they all began to act as such!

The similar thoughts that came to me then and since have filled a rather large book, so I will not try to set any more of them in writing here.

Who were Brother and I to suggest that much of the Catholic world had, for seven hundred years, failed to capitalize on one of its greatest treasures? Was I making a fool of myself, thinking that something I had said was said by the Holy Ghost, and that a simple little prayer this Brother had written was a revelation?

I immediately sat down at my desk and began to write. I recorded everything that had happened. I recorded my conversations with Brother, various little things I had noticed, and all my reactions. "I shall send all of these things to Father John (then at Middletown)," I determined, "and he can judge whether there is anything good or evil in them since he is at once Brother's confessor and mine."

The more I wrote, the more I saw things I had not seen before. Although a Carmelite cleric, I had never realized the importance of Carmelite traditions and of the fact that a Scapular wearer, by being affiliated to Carmel, was a member of a *Family of Mary* . . . a Family that had its roots, at least mystically, in the Old Testament. I saw that the early history of the Order was a Divine preparation of this Marian Society in which, to use the words of Saint Alphonsus Ligouri, "Men would need but stand silently to be sure of Salvation." And these thoughts frightened me, because I did not know then that they were the common knowledge of men

like Blessed Grignon de Montfort and Saint Alphonsus Liguori . . . and the Popes and of Catholics
in many countries. I thought they were new. "This is
indeed a mighty thing," I marveled, "and it certainly seems sound, since the Church does teach and
believe that one who wears the Scapular is, by the
power of Mary, assured of Sainthood."

Not being able to contain my élan of enthusiasm,
I rushed to the chapel to pour forth my whole being
before the tabernacle, lest my self-diffidence should
rise and rob me of this joy of spiritual discovery.

It was then that I felt sure that Brother had been
favored with a vision.

In the cornerstone above is a relic of the Holy House of
Nazareth. Left to right, the Brother - and I - and the
first Superior (Sr. Miranda) of the House of Prayer at
the U.S. National Centre of the Blue Army in Washington, N.J.

Accused of a Vision

Two DAYS after I received the morning offering from Brother and had decided that he had been favored with an apparition, I went down the corridor to his door, determined to find out just how much he did know about this Apostolate . . . and *how* he knew about it.

I little suspected in what strange manner this drama was to unfold.

Knowing in advance that my great obstacle would be Brother's fear of talking about anything concerning his own spiritual life, particularly about anything at all out of the ordinary, I laid a scheme.

It was difficult to get him to say "I think," or "It is my opinion," and it was almost impossible to get him to say "I have experienced such and such." I knew that my one way to draw him out was blank, direct questioning. He could never dissimulate; his reactions usually wrote themselves on his face.

The moment he opened his door, I said bluntly: "Brother, have you had a vision?"

He looked stunned. His face turned scarlet. Lines

27

of self-confusion, almost of pain, drew down the corners of his mouth. After a moment of silence, he stammered:

"Not in that way . . . not in that way," and he was trying to close the door.

My foot was in the way. An overwhelming curiosity had seized me and driven any other consideration out of my mind.

"What do you mean, 'not in that way'?" I accused. *"You did have a vision, didn't you?"*

Obviously getting a hold on himself now, Brother spoke more lucidly, but was very ill at ease. The door was not open more than four or five inches. The moment is as clear to me as though it had just passed.

"I might have had a vision," he said in a whisper, "and I might have had a dream. We mustn't believe in such things."

But I realized that *he did believe,* otherwise his reaction would not have been so strong. Undoubtedly he wanted to consult his spiritual advisor before giving the full consent of his will to what seemed a supernatural experience.

"Why not tell me?" I said. "After all, we are together in this." And then I told him, for the first time, what I had experienced when I spoke those words on the chapel porch.

He was silent.

"I'm writing everything out to send to Father

John, Brother," I whispered, "and you could share everything with me, go over what I have written to make sure that it is correct, and we can send it to Father John together."

"I'll see," Brother then replied, nervously, anxious to be rid of me. "I'll see."

I drew forth my foot, and he closed the door.

What I had said proved to be just the right thing. It was not more than fifteen minutes later that I heard Brother's knock at the door, and he invited me into a corner of the library to talk.

For once we had both forgotten the law of segregation.

"Frater Mathias," Brother began, after a conventional preface which I forget, "I saw a series of pictures so real that they woke me, leaving me with a feeling . . . a feeling that they were supernatural.

"First I saw myself opening a large wooden crate that had arrived downstairs, and in it were dishes and goblets as though for a banquet. The prior was there, and he said that a banquet was to be held at the Church of Our Lady of Peace, and then he left.

"Suddenly, I found that I was not unpacking dishes and goblets but mutilated statues of the Immaculate Conception . . . thousands of them . . . each one with broken arms or legs or head. I almost wept at the loss of so much beauty, and I set about gluing each statue together.

"To my amazement, I found that each one lacked some part.

"In the midst of all, I found a large and perfect statue of the Sacred Heart, unbroken.

"Then the scene changed and I found myself seated at a banquet table. It was on the lawn, beside the Church of Our Lady of Peace. A large platter of food had started at the head of the table and I noted that there was a kind of food there . . . one piece of it . . . that I had never seen before. The platter was passed all the way down the table, and no one took that strange piece. When the platter arrived at my place I said to myself: 'Well, no one else has taken this, so I might as well take it', and I put it on my plate.

"The moment I did so, a hand reached over and took it."

He sat silent a moment.

All the while my mind raced. I remembered the visions which led Saint John Bosco to his wonderful vocation. How very similar they were to the experience Brother had just narrated! But what did the pictures mean?

Brother broke in on my thoughts.

"When you asked me whether I had had a vision, Frater, I know you meant a vision of Our Lady, speaking and giving some message. And I will not say that what I have just described was supernatural, although I do think it was; and I awoke with the understanding that, lacking in our devotion to the Immaculate Conception is *moral union with Her, in all that we do.* I understood that if we do live through Mary by the Scapular, assuming, as it were, Her immaculate purity of heart and divine charity, *we shall quickly become united to the Sacred Heart.* And I understood that at the banquet table, where truths about Our Lady were passed down from century to century, this one was saved for general propagation until now, placed before me, and taken by you to be made known to the world."

Archbishop of Agra joins in worldwide coronation of Our Lady on May 13th, 1971. Hindus and Moslems participated with the Christians. "She will unite us all," His Excellency said.

CHAPTER SEVEN

Trial

FOR WEEKS I spent every spare moment working on the manuscript to be sent to Father John. I read as many books on the Scapular and the Sacred Heart as I could immediately obtain. Brother and I were frequently obtaining permission to talk together, and I learned a great deal. We worked out the message that seemed to have been entrusted to us. It can be told in a few paragraphs.

True sanctity is as natural as a flower, never turning its face from the sun, and ever pouring forth the perfume of doing the little things God wants of it on this earth, while depending on Him for all that it is. The safest flowers are those in Mary's garden, because She, over whom Satan has never had dominion, shields Her flowers against even the strongest storms. Moreover, Mary does more than this for Her flowers. She also places the sparkling glass of Her Immaculate Heart over each of them so that the Sun is drawn to them, and they grow strong, becoming more beautiful and reaching higher than the flowers in any other garden.

32

This is the doctrine of Saint Therese of Lisieux, the "Little Flower," who found that, having been brought back to life in her infancy, by Our Lady, she was transplanted to "Our Lady's garden of Carmel," where she reached a height of sanctity, in a few years, that dazzled the world.

During the following years I wrote repeatedly to Lisieux to find, from the living sister of Saint Therese, corroboration of this belief. And it came. And more came. Mother Agnes (Pauline) later wrote:

"We can only collaborate with you by our prayers in making known this wonderful message, but . . . it is our belief that *Saint Therese of the Child Jesus, who so much loves the Blessed Virgin, will aid in its realization . . . Our Saint will know, at the opportune time, to obtain the necessary aid for the work in question.*"

I had not spoken of aid . . . although aid, and almost miraculous aid, was going to prove necessary. And the Little Flower was indeed to obtain it.

Carmel and its Confraternity of the Scapular . . . Mary's Garden . . . are not bound by cloister walls. This is rather a garden that reaches throughout the entire world, to every corner of the world, and which is bounded by no walls other than a formula and the wearing of a sign: the formula of admission into Mary's Scapular Family, and the active profession of membership by the wearing of Our Lady's Scapular.

When the Carmelites left Mount Carmel and the Holy Land to move to the West for the first time, Our Lady appeared to Saint Cyril of Jerusalem and said: "Carmel is to be a light, not for Syria and Palestine alone; its rays must illumine the entire world."

Hardly had the Order . . . even then known as "The Family of Mary" . . . settled in the West, than Our Lady appeared to its Prior General and made Her most celebrated of all promises, the promise that extended the boundaries of Her garden to the ends of the earth:

"Whosoever dies clothed in this (the Carmelite Scapular), *shall not suffer eternal fire!"*

Since that time, the largest society in the world, after the complete Church herself, has come to be the Scapular Confraternity. The Scapular, with the Rosary, has come to be Catholicity's main expression of devotion to God's Mother. Speaking to the seminarians of Rome, Pope Benedict XV, of happy memory, said: "Let all of you have a common language and a common armor: the language, the sentences of the gospel; the armor, the Scapular of the Virgin of Carmel, which you all ought to wear . . . "

Some two hundred million Catholics wear it today.

And during the seven centuries that Catholics have enjoyed "Mary's Sacrament," as the Scapular is called, not everyone has overlooked its great value: that it unites us, morally, to Our Mother in

Heaven. Deepening this union, many have been able to reach true sanctity quickly and securely.

When the Scapular was placed over her shoulders, at the moment of investiture, Saint Theresa Margaret of the Sacred Heart swooned with joy, so much did she feel the intimacy of that bond with the Blessed Virgin.

Blessed Claude de la Colombière, S. J., coadjutor of Saint Margaret Mary Alacoque in making known the famous revelations of the Sacred Heart, said: "I would reproach myself where I to weaken your confidence in other devotions to Mary but, if Our Lady is propitious to those who practice other devotions, how much more propitious must She not be to those who wear Her holy Scapular!"

And corroborating this ascetical value of the Scapular, over and beyond its value as a certain sign of true devotion to Mary, and consequently of predestination, the Church does not praise Our Lady in the Mass on the Scapular Feast because She assured salvation, but because "On this day, through the holy Scapular, She took to Herself special children . . . *filios dilectionis.*"

The Scapular makes us more than just favored Catholics. It places us beneath Mary's Mantle. It keeps Her at our side, by a mutual contract. *She* has promised that we shall not die but in the state of grace, and *we* are living up to the conditions of the

Promise: membership in Her family, professed by wearing the Scapular.

A Scapular Apostolate would be nothing but the simple offering of what we do (as affiliates of Heaven's Queen) into Her hands, to be dispensed according to the intentions of the Sacred Heart. It would be *living* the special sonship which Our Lady conferred with Her Promise of assured salvation. In one sentence, it would be *an extending of the morning offering of the Apostleship of Prayer, through the day*.

Instead of just once *offering* all our actions to God in union with the Immaculate, we would *perform* them in union with the Immaculate. We would *advert* frequently, during the day, *to the fact that we,* beneath Our Lady's Mantle, are *morally united* to Her by a mutual contract.

Brother and I worked tnese thoughts out, bulwarked them with weighty quotations and elucidated them with examples, also recounting all that had happened. Then we sent it off to Father John, who was then Novice Master at Middletown, New York, and a Carmelite priest not only of deep spiritual perception, but one whose years and depth of soul had brought him an unfailing judgment in matters both spiritual and temporal.

I could hardly wait to hear from him. He *knew* Brother, and extraordinary though all these things had been, he would certainly believe, for one as near to God as that Brother could never be deceived. Besides, there was much logic in it all.

Two days later, Father John's reply came.

"Take any papers you have," he said, "and all the notes you have written and saved about these experiences, and burn them at once!"

Brother was older than I, and the weeks of supervision he had contributed to those pages were not weeks of enthusiastic endeavor, but of serious and very prayerful meditation. I was enjoying everything that happened because it was as though Butler's Lives of the Saints had suddenly come to life and I were in the midst of them. But Brother did not live in feathery idealism as I did, but in an idealism tried and plodding; he lived not so much by enthusiasm as by earnestness.

I cannot help admitting that I took the letter to him with a great deal of curiosity, wondering just how he would react to its humiliating message.

He read it through silently, his face revealing absolutely nothing to me. When he had finished, he asked:

"Will you bring down the papers, Frater?"

A short while later, every last sheet and scrap was blazing in the furnace.

CHAPTER EIGHT

Separation

NOT LONG after this, Brother was sent to a foreign mission, half way around the world. He had volunteered.

"My vocation, Frater," he said, "is to pray. Yours is to write and to do the work."

He is in that distant mission now, hoping he will be martyred, since he has begged God for martyrdom from the time of his earliest childhood. He does not know of this book, and he probably will never read it.

Before he left, he had two things to tell me.

First, the best kind of sanctity is the sanctity of spiritual childhood, as taught by the Little Flower.

Second, one should read, and re-read, the Little Flower's Autobiography.

It was understood that I was to launch a Scapular Apostolate, but I asked:

"What about the Apostolate of the Scapular?"

"Leave it in the hands of God," he replied. "If it is His Will, it shall be."

During the next two years, by utilizing spare time I

38

succeeded in learning to read a number of languages, and I took almost a thousand copy-book pages of notes on the Scapular. I do not hesitate a moment to say that this was largely through the power of Brother's prayers. In high school I had had only good averages. I failed the third grade in grammar school. But even while I was doing all this Scapular work, I was achieving unusually high averages in my college studies. One semester my average, to my own amazement, was over ninety-seven per cent.

One day, during these years, as a passing example of the thought I am trying to convey, I was walking down a corridor, at the end of which there was a fairly good-sized room in which hundreds of old books, habits, newspapers, magazines, pieces of soap, and what-not had accumulated. I was intent upon going somewhere, but a thought almost like a command cried: "There is something about the Scapular in that room of hodge-podge that you ought to read." I went in, and the first thing upon which my hand lighted was the back number of a small magazine in which I found an important article.

I kept Father John acquainted with all that I did. He did not object to my learning as much as I liked. As a matter of fact, he encouraged it, so long as I did not neglect my physical exercise and gave my best attention to my regular studies.

Moreover, after Brother went to the foreign mission, the Master of Professed was changed. The new

Master was an inspiration to me. I loved him and opened my heart to him, abiding by his every wish and following his every counsel. He was a true Carmelite . . . studious, prayerful, prudent, meditative, obedient, and passionate about anything that concerned the good of his Order.

In these days, that means a great deal. To be a good religious in any order, today, is to be a man of sterling character, of good nervous constitution, and of prayer. We are living in a worldly age . . . an age which definitely stresses the material rather than the spiritual. And the automobile and radio have brought religious houses closer to this more materialistic world.

So, between my letters to Father John and my daily contact with this fervent superior, I was guided in everything and I had never been, and never expect to be again on this earth, so happy.

One of the things I did in my spare time was bookbinding. I worked with an Italian priest, professor of Church History, to whom book-binding was a hobby and who loved books almost as much as life. This experience was to be valuable.

Also, the subject of Father Anastasius Kreidt is an interesting ray of side-light. Father Kreidt was the second person to join the Carmelites in this country. He later became Provincial, and built the first half of the big monastery in which I was professed.

During Father Kreidt's theological studies in

Rome, religious houses were confiscated by the government and the students were dispersed to the four corners of the earth. Father Kreidt went to Holland, to finish his studies, and before he returned to the United States he had lived in monasteries in several countries of Europe. He brought back with him a number of books on the Scapular devotion, in which subject he was vitally interested.

It was to read these books, which were collected in the monastery to which I belonged, that I became a linguist. At my disposal . . . due to the unplanned interest of Father Kreidt, who was my own granduncle! . . . I had the finest collection of books on the Scapular to be found in North America.

Father Kreidt also founded (and edited) two Catholic magazines, one in German: "Rundschau vom Berge Karmel"; and the other in English: "The Carmelite Review."

In these magazines, the main topic was the Scapular Devotion and from them I gathered many of the facts that made up those thousand pages of Scapular notes.

Towards the end of these years . . . at no part of which did Brother seem very far away . . . I had a premonition that I would not be a Carmelite. There was nothing outward to indicate that I might not realize my vocation, since I had my simple vows and I was happy actually to the point of bliss; but I nevertheless wondered what would

happen to my strange, perhaps extraordinary vocation . . . if I were not solemnly professed.

After three years of simple profession, I was refused admission to solemn vows and sent back into
the world.

The only explanation was: "God has not called
you to this state."

No one will ever know with what feelings I laid
aside my Carmelite Habit for the last time, having
worn it over my good suit until the last minute before
I had to leave.

What did the future hold?

Talking things over with Father John.

CHAPTER NINE

An Unexpected World

As THE train sped through the night, clicking off the miles to my home in South Jersey . . . home I had not seen for years and which somehow seemed remote . . . I knew that Brother was praying . . . probably in brilliant daylight . . . on the other side of the world. Above all, however, I knew that I was doing God's Will. It would be still a month before my vows would expire, and I was obeying my direct representatives of God.

After a few tears, for the first time in the many times that I had traveled by Pullman I fell into a sound sleep.

When I awoke the next morning in Atlantic City, and realized where I was, I began to experience a dangerous nervous tension. It was just the morning before that I had learned, so suddenly that the shock had not yet reached its climax, that I could not go on to solemn vows. And here I was, in America's pleasure city, five hundred miles from the building in which I had passed through adolescence and tried to shut the material world forever out of my life.

43

Even had I wanted to do so, I could not say much about my years in religion because I lived a very simple life there . . . a life very regulated and interior. During those youthful years . . . the longest years in a man's life . . . I was so engrossed with the task of self-education for the special vocation to which I began to believe that I was called, that things happened around me without my notice   It was pleasantry among some of my companions that I did not know the major news events.   For example, a nationally-famous bridge spanning a nearby river was brought tumbling down by a moving mass of ice one winter, and although the school was buzzing with the news, I was ignorant of it until two days after it happened.   I did not even notice things that happened right in the school itself.   My letters home were meditations on death and on the joy of loving God, with occasional descriptions of a hike, a hockey game (to which sport I was much attached, although I played with my ankles dragging on the ice), or the beauties of nature.   One news occasion presented itself when I was interpreter for three French priests from Quebec, who did not know English.   Another was when I lost my place following the music, while playing the pipe-organ at Benediction.   These few things, etching ever so small a groove in my tenor of study and prayer and more study, were innuendoes of a bliss of insouciance, in Mary's Habit.

And now I found myself, a grown man, in Atlantic

City. My family . . . which had been afflicted with those spiritual letters because I knew not how to write aught else . . . was waiting for me. And the world, which I had found unique happiness in leaving, had me back again.

From that day of my arrival in Atlantic City to the present day, so many things have happened to me that their narration would fill volumes. There was book-writing, several innocent love affairs, the launching of a nation-wide religious organization, marriage, book-publishing, travel, lectures, teaching school, consultation with the Under Secretary of State about joining the consular service, a start for France and from there to accept an offered professorship in England, and also the discovery that Brother had not been deceived . . . that it was indeed true that I was to transmit his message. And millions of American Catholics were to hear it in a much shorter time than I would have believed possible!

I do not think that all the things that have happened to me are important to readers of this "declaration." But I think that some of them . . . particularly interior experiences and reactions . . . were deliberately guided by Providence.

This may seem presumptuous, but it will readily appear that some of the things that happened were things of which I cannot be proud . . . and must, indeed, be ashamed. They are things which show the

devastating effect of spiritual unguardedness, in today's materialism, and which betray the weakness
of a man unguided.

So I shall start with this morning in Atlantic City
and narrate the "highlights" of the ensuing months
and years, insofar as they may bear on the message
which was left with me for development by our devoted, now far-away, Brother.

What might happen now would be the test of
his message.

After meeting in which Trustees of the Blue Army signed
contract for purchase of the Icon of Our Lady of Kazan...
which has been valued as high as three million dollars...
author presents copy of his latest book to Msgr. Colgan.

CHAPTER TEN

Suffering

MY FAMILY . . . particularly my father . . . constituted my main immediate interest.

My parents had given me much, and they had expected much of me. Now I was back on their hands, an utter disappointment to them. My mother wept for days. She did not know how to face the many friends with whom she had discussed her "Carmelite" son. One of her greatest joys had been to see me officiating as sub-deacon at Father John's jubilee of ordination and she had . . . oh, so proudly! . . . displayed pictures of the ceremony. And my father, a man of deep though gruff spirituality, had been counting the days to my ordination. He had asked nothing greater of Heaven than that one of his sons should be a priest . . . and I was his one hope, since my younger brother had married, and my older brother had never been inclined to clerical life.

I could not assuage my parents' disappointment and grief by telling them that this was all in God's plan . . . that a certain lay-Brother had had a *vision*

47

that involved me. They would have thought me insane. And I could not say: "Well, here I am and I shall go into your business, Dad, and make my way" ... which is the one thing that would have eased the trial for him.

I could take no definite step because I felt that I had a special work; even though I did not know how to go about that work!

This suffering was akin to torture. I loved my father so much that I could not bear to deal him such a dual blow ... defeating his hope for me, and yet refusing to enter his business although having no plan whatsoever for earning my way. And this latter fact caused me increased suffering because I felt that I was a man, and the thought of remaining *dependent on my parents,* like a child, so wrenched my pride that every fibre of my being rebelled.

What ... oh *what* did God want me to do?

My next three years were a struggle to find the answer to that question. I was to try one door after the other.

Of course, prayer was a principal refuge, but my mind lost little time ferreting out every possibility. Somewhere there was a door to my vocation, and I had to find it.

My initial plan ... and the one which I first presented to my father ... was to make a fortune by revealing to the scientific world a discovery I had made while studying Cosmology. I would write a book on my discovery, and the royalties would support me in spreading the Scapular Devotion . . . (which, I did confess, was my major interest).

My "scientific discovery" was not foolish. Indeed, it was not genuinely original; it had some adherents in the world of philosophy, although few in the world of physics. I felt that I could make philosophy and physics meet, and give a splendid working hypothesis for the entire science of Physics and Physical Chemistry. The only obstacle I could see was how to present my hypothesis in a manner that would be popular and financially satisfying.

Being quite practical, my father shook his head. I explained the hypothesis to him as best I could. It was a hypothesis that *explained* electricity, television, radio, the transmission of light, and many other natural mysteries. It stated: *Quantity is made up of positive and negative points of force.*

What makes a table or a wall or a stone *resist* pressure? "Quantity," I hoped to demonstrate, "which is nothing more than positive points of *force,* held in place by co-relative negative points of force." Electricity, I said, has no quantity because it is merely points of force in the pure positive or negative state. And the proof that something *without* quantity could *constitute* quantity is found in the fact that a bolt of lightning can split a giant tree as though it were a mighty steel ax.

The applications of the hypothesis were numerous.

Naturally, between a positive point of force and
a negative point of force, there is an electrical *field*.
And since all the world is fundamentally constituted
of these positive and negative points of force, this
field is universal. The undulations of this field constitute light and sound. Some undulations pass
through most densities of the universal field, but
there are certain densities through which they cannot
pass . . . for example, light passes through the field
that exists between the planets, but it is "undone", as
it were, by the field in a piece of wood. Radio can
transmit light and sounds by reducing them to a
strange undulation that is not undone by most fields,
and then reproducing and undoing the original undulations in a receiving set.

We would imagine that the five senses work simi-
larly. It is not an electrical impulse that rushes to
the brain when a man sees something. The optical
nerve is merely a receiving set, undoing the undulation of light, to which it is sensitve, and reducing it
to a new undulation: the type of undulation to which
the sense of touch reduces tactal sensation . . . the
same undulation to which the ear reduces sound . . .
the same undulation that causes all things sensed by
man to seem *one* sensation, and to be thus the tool
of his active intelligence.

The application that held greatest interest for me
was to the Eucharist. Our Lord's physical presence
under the appearance of bread would mean that the

points of force in His physical quantity were present, but that their *effect* was withheld by Divine Power . . . just as the fire that caressed the hand of Saint Bernadette was real fire, but its effect was suspended.

These are only a few of the many mysteries upon which this hypothesis seemed to cast light. And physicists seem to be coming more and more, from their experimental approach, to this very hypothesis which had so thrilled me from the philosophical approach. Accidents . . . such as color, odor, size . . . are modifications of quantity: modifications of the electrical field of a given substance. Essence is the entelechy that commands the points of force making up the Universe . . . and most essences were probably placed in a confused mass of these forces, with Divine plan, to evolve into the known Universe: a Universe designed to serve man.

Again, in the light of this hypothesis, how simple a mystery the glorified body becomes . . .

My mind reeled with satisfaction.

Yes, I did write the book. Quite a good-sized and unusual book, too, I thought at the time. Moreover, I later thought of a way of *proving* the hypothesis! I would take a dry cell battery, seal it to prevent escape of moisture, then weigh it before electricity was drawn from it, and weigh it afterwards. If the battery lost weight in the generation of electricity, then electricity . . . or pure force . . . might indeed be the constituent of quantity.

But I never submitted the book for publication, nor do I intend to do so. And I have never satisfied my curiosity about the comparative weight of a used and unused dry-cell battery.

When I was nearly finished with the book, the thought occurred: If you publish a book on a controversial subject . . . a book which will have both followers and opponents . . . what will be the effect of your book on the Scapular Devotion? Will not a great many people, particularly the intellectual opponents of your hypothesis, receive the Scapular book skeptically?

So, after long hours of thought and research, though sorely tempted . . . I passed by that first door.

John Haffert looks on as Father de Marchi, author of of books on Fatima, chats with Monsignor Colgan.

CHAPTER ELEVEN

A Lesson

DURING THE "scientist era" of these struggles at habilitation I came to know an unusually intelligent and capable scientific student, now with the staff of the celebrated *Institutum Divi Thomae*. She was a German refugee. And I allude to her acquaintance to open this anomalous, but highly important chapter. Her father was chief of staff of the Leoschutz Hospital . . . until Hitler promulgated a law which Catholic doctors were forbidden by the Vatican to obey.

That was the Nazi form of persecution.

It was not forbidden in Germany to attend Sunday school and Mass. But the youth *had to be present at Nazi exercises* during Mass and Sunday school. And Catholics were not forbidden to be Catholics, but if they did not abjure their religion and join the Nazi form of paganism, the government made their lives unbearable . . . as it is possible only for government officials to do.

In one town, over a period of twelve years, a pop-

53

ulation of thirteen thousand Catholics stopped going to church.

If these Catholics, immediately upon Hitler's rise to power, had been suddenly given the alternative of their lives or their religion, perhaps Germany would have had thousands of martyrs and her Catholic faith would be stronger today than evere.

But upon Hitler's rise to power, Catholics were assured of freedom. Hitler boasted that he was himself a Catholic.

Yet, insidiously, every assurance and every boast cloaked a new step to alienate Catholics from their faith.

In the event of similar persecution, Catholics of America would descend the same road down which so many Catholics in Germany have been drawn and pushed. England had a persecution of this nature once, and "Mary's Dowry" became a place where devotion to Her was considered an abomination. Russia had a similar persecution, and her new generation is godless.

This indirect form of persecution is diabolical in the extreme. And it is certainly the form of persecution of . . . "the latter times."

"If only German Catholics would stick to their Scapulars!" I thought to myself. "Our Lady has made Her promise and not any kind of persecution could pry a generation of Mary-clothed Catholics from their Sacraments."

I spent much time with the German refugees. The Doctor had letters from Cardinal Bertram (Primate of Germany) and from Cardinal Faulhaber, testifying to the sacrifice he (the Doctor) had made in leaving his high position in the German medical world rather than betray his Catholic obedience, and recommending that he be received warmly in the United States. It happened that my name was known to the Sisters of a metropolitan hospital, and I was able to give my friend a little aid. In return, I spent many hours learning from his lips the meaning of godlessness when it strikes in truly diabolical manner.

About this time (it was just before the occupation of Austria) an article appeared in an Austrian magazine called *Das Skapulier-Brücke* . . . "The Scapular Bridge."

To my amazement, the article was a description of *Brother's message!* Of course, the writer did not know Brother, but he had written:

"The Scapular is a bridge to Mary, and we should cross this bridge by imitating Our Lady, and thus our safety will be certain."

A few months later, the magazine in which this article appeared was suppressed. Austria had been struck.

I wrote an article myself, at this time, called *Zum Unbekannten* . . . "To the Unknown." It was a treatise on the Scapular Devotion, urging, by the most cogent arguments, that wherever there was danger of diabolical persecution, one should cling to Mary. I sent it to a friend in Vienna, with whom I had been corresponding for some time, and asked him to submit it to the Jesuit paper *Stimmen Aus Maria-Laach*.

I never again heard of the article. I never again received any correspondence whatsoever from Germany . . . not even my customary supply of magazines.

But, at this same time, I had a wonderful consolation.

While I was still in the monastery, I had sent a copy of Brother's "Morning Offering" to my family, suggesting that they recite it.

Knowing that I liked the prayer, and liking it very much himself, my father secretly sent away for some full-color holy-cards of Our Lady of the Scapular, and imprinted the offering. He sent me several hundred copies as a Feast-day gift.

I put the prayers away for the time, since my father had overlooked the necessity of an Imprimatur.

However, these few years later I was visiting a family in Philadelphia and had been invited to join with them in their night prayers, and after the seven members of the family had recited the Rosary I suddenly noticed that they had all taken out their Scapulars, and they began to recite that offering!

Three years before, my father had sent them a copy.

I cannot say what a feeling of consolation stole over me. It seemed almost as though I could hear all the Catholics of America pouring forth the offering of their great and menial tasks into the hands of Mary, for Her Divine Son. And when, at the words "She, whom Thou has appointed dispensatrix of the merits of Thy Precious Blood," they all reverently kissed Our Lady's Sign, it seemed that Our Lady had suddenly embraced them.

No persecution, of any nature, would be able to destroy the love of God in those hearts!

CHAPTER TWELVE

Our Lady's Book

WHILE TRYING various doors violently, and vainly, ranging from consideration of a chicken farm to actually studying for a Doctor's degree in Philosophy at Fordham University, from writing the already mentioned scientific treatise to actually seeking outright subsidy from several wealthy people, Our Lady was quietly achieving Her own plan.

A short time after I arrived home, among the many things I thought to try was teaching at the Carmelite seminary in Middletown, New York, where Father John . . . as was previously mentioned . . . was Master of Novices. I offered my services free of charge, to "fill in" until the real chance to realize my vocation presented itself . . . and also to pay the debt which I felt that I owed to the Order for my education.

My application was accepted, and I soon found myself teaching French and conducting a two-year course in *Scapularia* (the study of the Scapular Devotion) to applicants for the Carmelite priesthood. Soon my old happiness asserted itself. I was no

58

longer a burden on my family, because I did not immediately need clothing and I was being housed and fed. I had the constant companionship of Father John . . . in whom I could confide my every problem, particularly the problem of my vocation.

The seminary at Middletown . . . Saint Albert's College . . . is a very monastic, almost cold building. It has an air of implacable rigidity and solitude. It is just outside the limits of the town, surrounded by eighty acres of stream and lake and woodland . . . a sharp, stone and brick building that contrasts itself to the rolling terrain and nearby verdant mountains like a concrete Maginot fortress in a French forest.

I arrived just as the school term was beginning, and went to work immediately. I rejoiced at being once again in a monastic house, near the Blessed Sacrament at all times, able to seek advice whenever I needed it, brought back, in a word, into much of my old element.

Yet, it was really not my old element. There was one tremendous difference: My freedom. I could go and come as I wished. Strange above all, to me, was the experience of deciding I might go into town of an evening and go to a motion picture. In the seminary, I had only twice seen the city lighted at night. Indeed, I had only twice been outside the monastery walls at night: Once when I walked too far on a hike, and once when I was "showing the sights" to the three French priests from Quebec.

This element of freedom did not please me. It was the one thing to which I had to become accustomed. I had previously found all my happiness in knowing that whatever I did was exactly what God wanted of me because it was either dictated by my rule or by my superior. Now I did not know. To go to a motion picture did not seem quite right to me; yet I knew it was not wrong and I was fascinated every time I went. The motion picture seemed a wonderful marvel but, often, not an uplifting one. And this was only one of the things to disturb my peace of soul. I was no longer making my meditation. I had been so accustomed to "pop" out of bed at five in the morning and to be kneeling in the chapel for meditation twenty minutes later, that to get up at an hour of my own choice and to meditate at an hour of my own choice found me rising at an ever later hour, and meditating less and less.

I had not been trained for freedom; I was trained only for obedience. Under obedience to a Religious Order I had been strong; under freedom I was tempted to do all that was not forbidden by that broader rule of the ten Commandments.

But very few who have had the same experience of being prepared for a religious life, and then returning back to the world, have had the good for-

tune of being eased back into the laical state in the
same manner that I was. I had a monastic atmosphere, Father John guided me, the teaching of
Scapularia forced me to keep to spiritual meditation
to a considerable extent, and thus I became used to
the fact of being a layman, little by little.

As the snow was beginning to melt in the valley
around the college and to disappear from the mountains, during Lent of that first year at Saint Albert's,
I set to the task for which I had studied so hard:
the writing of "Her" book.

Teaching the facts of the Scapular Devotion to
the students for several months had greatly clarified
them in my mind, and I had my myriad notes thoroughly catalogued and unified. I made a rough outline . . . an outline I had dreamed about almost
five years. Almost ecstatically I began to fill it
out. Chapter followed chapter in rapid succession,
and Father John read each one and made various
constructive criticisms.

I had little confidence in myself as a writer; I had,
up to that time, written only three magazine articles
about the Scapular, and they had all been rejected.
But Father John expressed an ever-increasing surprise and interest as the complete manuscript took
shape.

I knew that it was not really my own work. I
knew I had collected all the facts, but I knew, too,
that those facts had come more or less providential-

ly into my hands. And sometimes, as I wrote, I felt that Our Lady was there. One time, particularly, Father John picked up what I had most recently written. Rather than sit silently while he read it, I decided to utilize the time and begin the last chapter. Father John said he didn't mind the clicking of the machine, so I rattled off the first few pages.

Hardly a word of that last chapter has ever been changed, and when Father John took it from me and read it as I continued to type, he suddenly looked up at me as though he had been present at a quasi-revelation.

And I think he had. For that last chapter is the message from Brother, who had said: "If it is to be, God will see to it."

The reader probably knows that *Mary in Her Scapular Promise,* as the book was called, was received with enthusiasm by the Catholic public.

And thus Our Lady took care of the work, and of me: by easing me into the laical state, giving me a perfect environment for the writing of Her book, and giving me Father John to be my constant companion and to mould me for whatever She had for me to do.

Before I left Middletown, two years after I had gone there, I had arrived at a new character.

However, a priest had become available for teaching French at the College, and certainly a book would not support me. This book particularly would

Father John

not support me, because I resolved before it was published that any proceeds from it would go to its further propagation.

Should I now become a priest? Or should I, with this job done, go into my father's business? What about the other books I felt I should write: Might I beg until they were accomplished? I was not needed at Saint Albert's, and the old problem was there again:

What was to become of me? Was the task accomplished?

CHAPTER THIRTEEN

The Lecturer

THE FIRST affair of the heart, the struggle about my priestly vocation, the solution of my problems by a Bishop, are all so jumbled with my belief that I might support myself by giving lectures that I want to segregate them all from that most interesting and significant of all the doors I tried: the rostrum.

My first lecture was given at Immaculata College, about forty miles outside Philadelphia, the College with the fourth highest scholastic rating of all the Eastern Colleges for girls. The lecturers there were usually such persons as Father Gillis, Frank Sheed, Michael Williams, and so on. I wrote as professional a letter as I could muster, offering my services for the cost of expenses, explaining that I wanted to make known that age-old, but somewhat forgotten devotion of the Brown Scapular.

The fact that *my sister* was a well-liked student in the College could have had something to do with the fact that I was invited. Besides, she *did* go and fairly *plead* to the College President that he would not regret the invitation . . .

Anyway, as a recent ex-Carmelite, to whom public speaking was a class-room lesson and to whom college girls were an unknown and frightening quantity, I found myself . . . by some magic . . . pacing the marble floor outside the Immaculata auditorium. The buzz of feminine chatter from three hundred students sounded through the door like the murmur of a Metropolitan Opera House audience. My clammy hands were keeping each other nervous company behind my back, and I stared vacantly into space as I tried to look nonchalant. The priest who was to introduce me was late.

But Our Lady was there. For some reason, I seemed cut out for an easy path in this new work. When my master of ceremonies arrived . . . it was genial, self-composed, Father Francis Walsh. He took one look at me, put his arm over my shoulders, and asked quietly: "Well, what do you want me to say about you, other than that you've written a book on the Scapular and that Monsignor Sheen has written the preface?"

Very few people knew that the book had just been written, and Monsignor Sheen had merely consented to write the preface, so I knew my sister had been at work and I immediately ceased to feel like a stranger.

I have lectured literally hundreds of times since that first day, but I never received any other introduction like the one then made by Father Walsh. It was such a wonderfully fabricated "build-up" that I actually felt that it was I who was doing Immaculata College a favor.

The lecture was well-liked and I was invited back to give it again the following year, and I was given a good deal more recompense than my expenses. Moreover, when I had spoken the first time, only three in the entire audience were wearing the Scapular; and when I spoke the second time, almost every girl in the College was wearing it.

This spiritual and financial success encouraged me very much. I felt that here was certainly the solution to my problem: I could lecture once a week, and have the rest of the time for writing books! Surely, considering all the Catholic schools and Colleges in America, it would not be difficult to obtain fifty-two lecture invitations a year!

The next invitation came from the Redemptorist seminary, at Esopus, New York.

I had bought myself a second-hand car for fifty dollars . . . subsidized by my father, of course. The trip to Esopus (where I expected to speak before students of high school or early College age) was filled with anticipation and the thrill of owning and driving a car. Each curve I turned, each car I passed, each time I halted the miraculous machine and started it, were inexplicable thrills. It was a massive Nash sedan, 1929 vintage, weight two tons, plush seats inside and shining brilliantly outside . . . although several years behind the current style. And the scenery along the Hudson left me spell-bound. As the car rolled up and down the concrete pavement that seemed to rush southwards under the wheels, my heart sang. "And to think," I said to myself, "that I'm having all this fun and yet I'm traveling to do Our Lady's work . . . to spread Her message among young followers of Saint Alphonsus, one of my favorite saints!" No matter how I looked at the situation, it was blissful.

Delayed by ignorance of the road, I arrived at Esopus much later than planned. It was dusk, and I was scheduled to lecture in just an hour. When I drove into the courtyard, a strange feeling came over me. The place was tremendous. It seemed like a miniature city. A priest came out to greet me and took my bag. Priests seemed to be everywhere I looked. I was shown down endless corridors to the Bishop's suite, which had been prepared for me. I was installed, and the young priest said: "Our Father Wuenschel will be down to entertain you until lecture time; the Rector was called away."

Left alone, for some reason that "old" feeling came over me. This was not a petit seminaire, as I had supposed, but it was a major seminary! And here I was . . . a layman, barely old enough even to be ordained, honored in the Bishop's suite and expected to lecture to priests! Certainly they had thought me a much older person. And Father Wuenschel . . . surely I knew him! . . . he was the famous Redemptorist lecturer on the Holy Shroud, whose magazine articles and public talks were known throughout the country.

A few minutes later my worst fears were confirmed. A knock came on the door, and it was indeed Father Wuenschel, S. T. D., professor of Theology and expert on the Holy Shroud. And I soon knew that I would be addressing an audience of advanced seminarians and of from sixty to seventy priests! I almost melted on the spot.

But again Our Lady was with me . . . or would it be better to say She was with the Redemptorists?

Father Wuenschel told me that the seminary was celebrating a jubilee of Saint Alphonsus, their founder. And I knew, while the prospective audience probably did not know, that everything in the tomb of Saint Alphonsus . . . his flesh, his episcopal robes, everything corruptible . . . had decomposed with a single, marvelous exception: the Saint's Brown Scapular. And I had so loved the *Glories of Mary* that I had read it in four languages as my means of mastering a Marian vocabulary in those languages. Thus a new talk began to formulate itself in my mind . . . punctuated with a fervent "Saint Alphonsus, help me!", or "Mary, don't fail me!"

When I walked down the aisle to the rostrum, through a sea of Redemptorist habits, my knees knocked against each other at every step.

"You all have probably read," I began in a high-pitched, strained voice, "the book by A. J. Cronin, called *The Citadel*."

Everyone apparently felt sorry for me.

"Well," I struggled on, "you will remember the layman in the book who specialized in the study of tuberculosis. He didn't become a doctor, because he wanted to give all his time to tuberculosis . . . and a doctor has to study so many things he cannot usually afford to spend all his time on one thing. And you will remember," and here I made a mighty effort to lower my voice an octave or so, while fishing for the next word because this introduction had just occurred to me, "You will remember that he became such an expert on tuberculosis that all the doctors went to him for advice.

"Now I have not become a priest, as you have done, but I have devoted my time to specializing in the Scapular Devotion."

As I said this, it became apparent to me that I was comparing myself to an expert, and my emotions, of sudden realization and of dismay, were so plainly written on my face that the whole audience broke into a hearty laugh, and I laughed with them.

That mutual laugh was like magic. It broke down a thousand barriers, and I honestly believe that I have never given a more natural talk than the one that followed. It was an exposition of the Scapular Devotion with frequent allusion to Saint

Alphonsus and his writings and, including the hour of questions, it lasted two hours.

I knew in my heart that after the experience of lecturing on the Scapular to College girls, of whom I was afraid, and then lecturing to Priests, of whom I was in awe, that I would not be dismayed by any other audience.

And as one of the effects of this lecture at Esopus, I learned that a Redemptorist at the Catholic University of America, two years later, remarked to a Carmelite student that he had heard a layman lecture on the Carmelite Scapular at Esopus, and that he had resolved to study and pray to become a great missionary, since a layman could speak with so much zeal and effectiveness on a spiritual subject.

However, that same night that I lectured at Esopus, I had a great deal of cold water thrown on my awakening fire of enthusiasm for lecturing as an *economical* enterprise.

After the talk, Father Wuenschel had addressed a few words to the audience, among which he said: "When it becomes known that this lecture we have just heard is available, it will be in demand from Coast to Coast." So, back in the solitude of the Bishop's suite, I eagerly asked him:

"Do you really think the lecture will be in demand?"

"I really do," Father Wuenschel answered, sensing that I was seeking genuine advice. "I am constantly called to lecture on the Holy Shroud, and you are lecturing on something of even greater importance and interest, and your lecture is excellent."

"I'm glad to hear that," I replied, "because I love the work, and the talks not only help to accomplish my desire to spread knowledge of the Scapular, but they will also pay my way."

"Well, that's where you're wrong," Father Wuenschel interposed. "They will not pay your way. If I were not supported by my Order, I would have starved as a lecturer. Fees barely cover expenses."

My heart sank.

Was this, the most attractive of all the doors yet before me, also to be passed by?

Left: The author speaking at the International Seminar on the Immaculate Heart of Mary in Fatima, August of 1972, following the International Marian Congress in Zagreb.

CHAPTER FOURTEEN

Nearing the Right Door

THE VOCATION I considered most during all this time was the vocation to the priesthood. That vocation would have solved most of my problems. It would have brought security, peace of mind, satisfaction to my parents, the realization of a childhood dream, the practice of the one vocation for which I had been educated.

But, as a priest, I had to ask myself whether I would be able to write and go about lecturing on the Scapular. Besides, if God had wanted me to be a priest . . . much though I myself desired it . . . would He have sent me into the world almost on the eve of ordination?

If I became a secular priest, as an assistant-pastor I could certainly not lecture around the country; as a pastor, I would be still further bound . . . having every soul in the parish on my conscience. And, in religious life, how could I know what I might be permitted to do? It might happen that I would be found most acceptable for teaching, or

72

for something seemingly more important than the
spreading of one Marian devotion.

Until my doubt was finally settled authoritative-
ly, I was constantly on the verge of casting hesitation to the wind and applying for admission into
the Society of Jesus; the Jesuits had taken an important role in the promotion of the Scapular Devotion, and they encouraged specialization.

When I first went to Middletown and had a long
conference with Father John . . . who knew, of
course, the complete nature of my problem . . .
Father John was as much bewildered at the number
of various possibilities as I was myself. He was inclined to feel, however, that I should by all means
keep myself free for the founding of the Scapular
Apostolate.

That was how I first knew that Father John approved . . .

Meanwhile, the book, *Mary in Her Scapular
Promise* became ready for publication. And this
gave me my chance to express the idea that had long
been closest to my heart: A Scapular Organization.

My father had a small publishing business, and
in that I saw my main opportunity.

"Dad," I said, "you finance this new book and I
will earn a partnership in the enterprise by doing
all the work . . . even proof-reading, press supervision, sales. We can publish it under a Scapular
trade name, since spiritual book-publishing will be

new to you. People will read the book and will then be moved to become apostles of the Scapular, and they will write to us for further literature . . . pamphlets, leaflets, books, holy cards, prayer-manuals, scapulars. Thus a following will develop, and we can use our address as a place where the Scapular miracles . . . that happen daily . . . can be recorded. The final step will be the publication of a magazine called *The Scapular*."

I reasoned that, in this manner, the propagation of the Apostolate was assured. The main requisite was the trade name, address, and possibly some symbol which people might identify with the movement.

But my father, looking at the proposition from a practical businessman's point of view, refused to touch it. Yes, if I liked, he would publish the book, but only under his established name; it would jeopardize the success of the book to publish it not only under the name of an unknown author but also under the name of an unknown publishing house, obviously founded for that one book. Besides, he owned two successful magazines and he knew . . . as I did not . . . that magazines which support themselves solely on subscriptions are apt to lose money for years before they are successful. And as for selling ten-cent articles by mail . . . that was positively a project for financial disaster.

If my father knew then what the reader knows,

after reading the past few chapters, probably he would have risked financial disaster. But he did not know these things, for the simple reason that I did not have the ability to describe them to him. The feeling that Scripture expresses "a prophet is without honor in his own country" was like a seal on my lips.

Unfortunately, as a consequence, my father looked upon my attitude towards life with great concern. He thought I had become lazy and unwilling to work, and as I presented one seemingly inane idea after another . . . all avoiding the priesthood or preparation for some acknowledged position in the business world . . . he wondered that I might even be his son. He would have liked nothing better, in lieu of my becoming a priest, than that I go into the business that had taken him years to build.

This suffering he underwent was almost as great as my own. And it was augmented at this time by the death of his mother, and by my sister's longing to leave home to become a Carmelite nun. My sister had always been his "pet." He could not consider life without her, and the walls of a cloister seemed to him almost like the walls of death . . . so isolating were they. I was the one who had fostered my sister's vocation and I was urging, strongly, that she realize her longing.

Then suddenly everything changed.

I was wondering how my father ever bore his multi-weighted trial as equably and unselfishly as he did, because he would have died either to prove his devotion to my sister, or to solve his concern for me.

But one morning, when he came down to breakfast, he seemed fairly to radiate a strange peace, as though the entire trial had been suddenly lifted from his shoulders.

My sister entered the convent, not only with the full consent he had been so reluctant to give, but with his ardent aid and fervent blessing. In Carmel, like a soul freed from the cage of the world into the regions of Heaven, she found unspeakable happiness, and she was given the name Sister Therese of the Queen of Carmel.

Furthermore, the Scapular Press was founded, and with its own symbol . . . to which point my father had *particularly* objected because he felt that if the Scapular Press was to be the spiritual book division of the Garden State Publishing Company, that it should work under a Garden State symbol. Again, too, the permission was more than an acquiescence; it carried full cooperation.

Somewhat sheepishly, my father later confessed the reason for his sudden complete change and peace of mind.

"It seemed to me that my entire life," he said, "was a hopeless muddle of odds and ends. And then the lives of you and your sister suddenly appeared in the muddle like magic keys, and the odds and ends formed a radiant mosaic of the Blessed Virgin."

I drew up the title page *for Mary in Her Scapular Promise* and, to get a rough concept of the page, I roughly scribbled a few circles where the seal would be, and put the words of our motto around the scribbled lines. Then I drew a blending plan for the chapter heads and left both of them on my father's desk.

My father did not comment on them but, a few days later, to my surprise he brought home an artist's drawing. He passed it to me and said, quite naturally:

"I had our staff artist draw up that seal, John. I personally think he did a good job, although I was afraid he was going to have difficulty with that figure of the Blessed Virgin. What do you think of it?"

I took the drawing, my eyes wide with amazement and curiosity, and there, copied from where I had merely scribbled some lines, I saw a beautiful image of the Blessed Virgin standing over the world with the Scapular, as though to clothe it and, radiating from behind the clouds on which She stood and which seemed to support the world in space, was the rising sun. Encircling the picture, in Latin, were the words: "The world in the arms of Mary!"

(See illustration at the end of the chapter)

If I had racked my brain, I could not have conjured up a more ideal symbol of the Scapular Apostolate: Our Lady of the Scapular clothing us in Her Sign and, seeing His Immaculate spouse in us, the Spirit of God rising up to illumine us to Divine Life. The symbol was actually a *picture* of the message in *Mary in Her Scapular Promise.*

"O might all the world receive this message," I thought, "and approach, through Our Lady and with Her Sign of Alliance, to Her Divine Son!"

"The artist carefully copied your drawing, John," my father broke in on my silence which he had presumed was disapproval. "He added only those few clouds around the world to give it the idea of floating in space."

"But, Dad!" I exclaimed, "I didn't draw any picture! I merely scribbled a few hapless circles to see how a seal would have looked on the page!"

And little did either of us think, as we stood there in silent awe, that only a few years later this wonderful symbol would have been printed millions of times.

At any rate, we were satisfied that the Scapular Press was a step in the right direction.

CHAPTER FIFTEEN

Wealthy Widow

THE ENTIRE skein of mystery seemed to be solving itself in a magical manner, but there were still many loose threads. It would take possibly four or five years for *Mary in Her Scapular Promise* to create a following, and the Scapular Press could not disseminate literature on an unknown subject. Indeed, the growth of the Press would be a long and slow process, and probably for several years would not require my full time.

My father felt that I should become a priest. "I'll carry out the Press idea," he said, "and you can tell me what to do, if your priestly station hinders you from participating yourself."

So the old trouble was back again: Indecision.

Then I thought of my Bishop. I did not have a pastor, properly speaking, because I was traveling about giving lectures and had not settled down. But the Bishop who had given the Imprimatur to the Scapular book was unquestionably my religious superior . . . and to obey him would be to obey God's will! Furthermore, by delightful coincidence, I

79

knew His Excellency . . . for the Bishop had read *Mary in Her Scapular Promise* himself to give it the Imprimatur, and he had been so deeply moved by it that he called me to the Chancery office to tell me so.

Bishop Eustace, of Camden, probably needs no introduction in these pages, because he was long a professor in the New York Archdiocesan seminary, and his reputation for sanctity and wisdom had traveled the Eastern States. He had tender and intelligent blue eyes, and a modest manner which no one who met him could readily forget. When I first met him, I felt that I had no secret from him; before the brief interview was over I had told him the secret I had until then most carefully guarded: Brother's vision. He listened gravely and understandingly, and then said: "Well, son, you have certainly made a wonderful start in your vocation with this book."

So now I was going back to him to finally settle the doubt . . . at least the doubt about the priesthood.

The Bishop had just been in his diocese two years and he was so deluged with work that he said his Divine Office immediately after his Mass in the morning because often, at night, due to utter fatigue he could hardly carry himself. His primary devotion was to Mary Immaculate, and he had dedicated his diocese to Her and had placed the names of all his priests in a golden reliquary about the neck of the statue of the Immaculate in his home, on the staircase where he passed it morning and evening.

"Will you forgive me for taking your time, Your Excellency," I stammered, "but it will not take long, because I have carefully prepared what I am going to say, and I think you are the only one who can help me."

When I first presented my problem to Bishop Eustace, the month of May was just about to open.

"I am going to pray every day in May, son," he said, "for Our Lady's guidance; and I want you to pray with me. Then, at the end of May, I'm sure we shall find the answer. Meanwhile, I want you to lecture on the Scapular in my diocese. I'll have an itinerary of the important parishes made up for you."

A short time later, a new development appeared on the already difficult scene.

I was lecturing to a select audience at a convent of Third Order Carmelites in Philadelphia. The community of nuns formed the major part of the audience, and the few lay people had been individually invited by the sisters.

Unknown to me, the smart-looking young lady whom I particularly noticed among the invited guests was a well-to-do widow, who had read *Mary in Her Scapular Promise* and had been so moved that she had immediately decided that she would, for the rest of her life, spend much of her time and fortune in making the Scapular more known. She had been invited to the lecture at her own urgent request.

It may seem disappointing to have such an interesting part of this story shortened, but suffice it to say that before the end of May I had come to know this young lady well. She was a daily communicant, very devoted to Our Lady, well educated, tall, smartly dressed, attractive. And after that short time she seemed to be in love with me.

When I went back to see the Bishop at the end of the month . . . exactly on the Feast of Mary, Mediatrix of All Grace . . . I was bursting with the news, but had decided to wait and see what the Bishop had decided with reference to the priesthood.

"Son," the Bishop said with an air that immediately told me he had come to a decision, "I think you are called to the laical state. The fact that you have a serious doubt about the matter primarily brought me to this decision, but the value of your work as a layman . . . the power of a layman's message . . . has given it strength." Then he asked: "What is your attitude towards marriage, son?"

"Well," I answered, "I thought that should you decide that I was not to be a priest that I might marry were my work such that I was kept in one place most of the time, but that I should not marry if my work called for much travel."

The Bishop was evidently much pleased with this

answer. Then I felt that it was opportune to tell him about the widow.

He received the news calmly, and then said:

"Well, son, proceed very cautiously in this matter."

So I did. I saw a good deal of the lady in question, and every time I saw her I was seeking faults. All in all, I was much pleased with what I found and finally thought that I must have reached the stage of love. So I wrote to the Bishop . . . not having the courage to make a personal visit . . . and told him I thought it was "the real thing," and that my parents made no objection. His answer seemed to hesitate, but based on my parents' attitude, he gave his blessing.

Plans for the wedding were set that very June for the following October 7th, Feast of the Holy Rosary. In other words . . . a dyed-in-the-wool celibate was contemplating marriage within four months!

Few will know what this means. Perhaps that is why the Bishop hesitated. Education to celibacy can be very powerful; it can almost completely alter one's outlook on life. And I now began to experience this fact. I simply was not conditioned for marital life; like an instrument pitched to a different key, it was going to take more than wishing to bring me in harmony with a way of life I had never contemplated for myself.

My fiancée did not altogether understand me. For

instance, she thought it queer that I should object to, of all things, a new Cadillac. We quarreled. And it soon dawned on both of us that I was neither ready for marriage nor ready for comfort, good though both of us appeared in each other's eyes.

And thus another door was passed by.

In 1946, Pope Pius XII crowned Our Lady of Fatima as QUEEN OF THE WORLD. One year later the Pilgrim Virgin statues left Fatima to encircle the world as though the Queen desired, said the Holy Father, "To make visits to all her dominions." In this picture the Bishop of Fatima (enlarged insert) blessed pilgrim statues which toured America and traveled to Moscow. Also seen are Rev. L.G. de Oliveira, O. Carm., and Madame John Wiley (wife of U. S. ambassador), holding crown.

CHAPTER SIXTEEN

Interlude

WITH THE help from Bishop Eustace, who handsomely recompensed me for the Scapular lectures in his diocese, and through the good fortune of having a succession of lecture invitations from many quarters, I found that my way more or less paid itself; I was even able to buy some new clothes, despite the fact that I had to meet the cost of continually traveling about. *Mary in Her Scapular Promise* was published a little more than a year after I had completed the manuscript, and it found immediate popularity. Four months after the date of publication it took first place among the best-selling spiritual books. Naturally I found many doors open to me.

One of these doors was that of Saint Leo's Abbey, in Florida, about thirty miles from Tampa. Having learned my problem through correspondence, the Abbot graciously invited me to come and stay, free of charge, as long as I liked.

I went. And were it not for a sizable schedule of lectures in Southern Louisiana, I might be there yet.

In the morning, after Mass, I did spiritual reading beneath palms, on the shore of an azure lake. Then I went to my room . . . a wonderfully severe and studious room, with high ceiling and monastic furniture, books, my little radio that brought all the Spanish stations from nearby Cuba, and windows that looked over a beautiful green plaza, through a lane of palms, and down an orange-planted slope to the blue lake. It was something one would dream about. I studied and worked at my notes in the morning, and in the afternoon I went out and worked around the grounds . . . cutting grass (of which there seemed to be acres), picking up the fallings from the palms, pulling Spanish moss from sagging oaks, raking debris, carrying stones for a wall being built by one of the priests (the Prior, no less), and sundry other physical tasks.

It was during this time that I particularly studied the Scapular Medal question, from every conceivable angle. The results filled pages, which I digested into an article which appeared a short time later in the American Ecclesiastical Review.

Saint Leo's Abbey was so interesting to me that even though I have pledged myself to write in these pages about only those things which bear upon the fulfillment of Brother's trust, I cannot help but tell one little story about my arrival there.

I had lectured in West Palm Beach, and was traveling across the Everglades in my 1934 Ford (for which I had traded the more antiquated Nash).

The strange, tropical scenery held me utterly captivated. I saw wild ducks gliding undisturbed in the
stream beside the road as I whizzed by. And it was
open season! And everywhere along the way I saw
egrets, and white and gray cranes of a variety un-
familiar to me. I almost wrecked the car the first
time I saw a pelican. I was driving at about fifty
miles an hour when suddenly, whizzing down from
the sky with cavernous jaws, this strange beast hit
the surface of a passing lake, like a plane in crash-
landing. When I came to myself, I was driving on
the *left shoulder* of the road!

This fascination with tropical vegetation and ani-
mal life reached its peak when I started to drive
through the citrus groves. There, hanging from the
trees just as naturally as though they had been carefully hung there from the bins of Consolidated
Stores, Inc., were grapefruit, oranges, and tangerines
. . . mile after mile, as far as I could see!

I stopped the car many times. Whenever I saw
trees hanging over the road, with the fruit just about
to drop, I got out to help nature along . . . and with
the decision of not going to Saint Leo's Abbey empty-
handed. I was going to take enough fruit for the entire community.

Before dark, the seat beside me was piled to the
top with grapefruit, oranges and tangerines, and
every time I made a left-hand turn, several dozen
oranges rolled down an improvised cardboard bar-

rier and piled around my feet. I soon began to regret my enthusiasm.

Two flat tires added to my delay. But finally, seven miles off the main road, in the pitch dark of night, I belatedly drove through the gates of the Abbey.

I had expected to find one large building. Instead, looming in the darkness in close proximity there were at least *five* buildings.

"Now where on earth, at this hour, am I supposed to go?" I asked myself, driving up and down the palm lanes that twined around the buildings endlessly.

I finally determined that the building with the plaza in front was the Abbot's building, because it looked large enough for the whole Benedictine Order. So I parked the car, draped my coat over the "surprise" load of fruit, blocking back a few oranges that held the door from closing, and then climbed the steps of the utterly dark Abbey.

The front door was open. It led into what seemed to be a tiled court, and I could gradually discern rooms on either side and large double doors at the end. I groped my way towards those doors, knowing that the Community undoubtedly lived on the second floor.

I did not, for some reason, feel like an interloper; but rather as though I belonged there.

The two doors indeed led to a staircase, and a faint light gleamed from somewhere above.

So I went up.

The light was from the room of one of the monks, down a long corridor to the left. I walked down, marveling that all the doors of the cells were screen doors, and knocked on the door through which streamed the guiding light. It was, as I found later, the Prior's room. And it was the Prior who heard me say, as he was pouring over some financial statements: "Pardon me, Father, are you the Abbot?"

The next day, I somehow slept through the five-o'clock Mass. But one of the monks had come to light the fireplace in my room, and at some equally ungodly hour, with banging eyes, I was led to the dining room for breakfast.

The dining room had what a New Yorker would call "plenty of atmosphere" . . . with solid wooden tables, low ceilings, dark walls, and the monks gathered silently with their hoods over their heads, each at his own place. The Abbot's chair . . . an immense armchair with His Lordship's coat of arms blazoned on its crest . . . was vacant. The Abbot was away on business, and he had forgotten to tell the Prior anything at all about me . . . with the result that the Prior treated me like an Auxiliary Abbot, "just in case." By exception, talking was allowed at breakfast.

The meal started with half a grapefruit, and I immediately thought of the treasure I had brought half way across Florida to the Community: enough citrus fruit for *several* breakfasts!

When we had finished, the Prior asked me if I would like to see the grounds.

He took me out into the early morning sunshine and there . . . almost as far as I could see . . . were citrus trees! "Are they all orange trees?" I gasped. "No," the Prior replied, "there are all sorts of citrus trees here. The factory, where they are cleaned and packed for shipping, is over there," and he pointed to a large building to the east. "You see," he added, "we support ourselves for the most part by raising citrus fruit."

A few days later, placed conspicuously on the side of the main road where some tourist could not miss them, was a pile of slightly battered grapefruit and oranges.

Cardinal Van Roey of Belgium Congratulates Monsignor Colgan. "The Blue Army is the only completely spiritual movement in the Church here," the Cardinal said.

CHAPTER SEVENTEEN

Attitude

EVERYWHERE I went, I lectured.

And it seemed to me that in both North and South the word "Scapular" was familiar to my listeners, but that its meaning was obscure.

This general ignorance of the Scapular everywhere made the talks "amazing," as several commentators remarked. But it was indeed myself who was amazed . . . amazed by the fact that anything as near to the Catholic heart, anything as highly indulgenced and as old and miraculous and acclaimed by saints and Popes, could be unknown to any Catholic, particularly in Catholic institutions of learning. And finding this ignorance so widespread, I could not help but fear a little for any quick success with the apostolate I had been trusted to launch. In general, I think I might even say that some audiences I have addressed were at first not only skeptical, but even slightly antagonistic. I somehow felt that I had far overestimated, in my own mind, the appreciation American Catholics have of the Blessed Virgin.

Consider the man who says: "Cut out non-essentials! We hear too much talk about the Rosary and these devotions. What we need is the Sacraments, because they're the essential things!"

Is not such a man poorly informed? And, unfortunately, is it not possible even for a priest to be so poorly informed, owing to a stripped-down curriculum in our seminaries?

The Popes have gone to great pains to point out that we NEED these devotions; Pope Leo XIII, for example, wrote *encyclicals* on the Rosary, and Pope Benedict XV, great Pontiff of World War I, told the *seminarians of Rome* of two essentials: "Let all of you," he said, "have a common language and a common armor: the language, the sentences of the *Gospel;* the armor, *the Scapular of the Virgin of Carmel"* . . . that is, let all of you have Christ as his life, and Mary as his protectress!

Catholic life must include devotion to Mary . . . the Mother Who consented to the Incarnation and who suffered beneath the Cross for us . . . or it will die. The surest way of insuring that any man or woman will go to the Sacraments . . . the source of Grace . . . is to place his or her hand in the hand of the Blessed Virgin. And the surest way to kill interest in the Sacraments, or to insure that the Sacraments will be little appreciated, is to say that Mary is non-essential.

Mary is so absolutely essential that NO CATHO-

LIC CAN BE SAVED WITHOUT BEING DE-
VOTED TO HER.

Therefore it must wrench the heart of anyone who
loves Our Lord to hear an educated Catholic say
that devotions to His Mother are stressed too much.
It was that we might truly find Him that He said,
as He died on the cross, "Behold thy Mother!" For
as He is necessarily all Justice by His Divine Nature, Our Lady is all mercy by Her motherly nature.
When Our Lord would say "This soul is faithless to
Me . . . My time is not yet come" (as Mary asks
Him to change the water of faithlessness in someone's heart to the warm wine of love) then She would
still whisper some little counsel in our hearts that we
might prepare for His coming . . . because She knows
that Her Divine Son can refuse Her nothing She
asks of Him and has, indeed, made Her the Mother
of men for that very reason.

It is possible to become frightened at the sight of
many Latins almost worshipping the Virgin, attending Mass *only* on Easter and the Feast of the Brown
Scapular, and neglecting all other church duties.

However, it is not right to throw out devotion to
the Blessed Virgin, or even to minimize it, simply because some Catholics *may have what Saint Grignon
de Montfort describes as false devotion.*

It is often true that a man will be strong in charity
and weak in humility. And should we *minimize* charity to foster humility? Or rather should we not *be-*

gin with charity to foster humility, by pointing tactfully to the fact that humility is a *form* of charity, because pride offends God and man?

It is shortsighted, therefore, to omit instructions on devotion to Mary . . . and particularly on the Scapular . . . for fear of detracting from "the more important facts . . . the Mass, the Sacraments." Where devotion to Mary is strongest there is a good groundwork for education to the Sacraments. And where there is not sufficient devotion to Mary, there is probably no religious solidity whatsoever.

Was it overemphasis on the part of Heaven when, in 1929, only *one* corruptible thing was found preserved in the tomb of Saint John Bosco: his Scapular? Was it overemphasis on the part of Hell when Satan was forced to admit, to the Venerable Francis Yepes, that one of the three things that most torments the damned is the Brown Scapular? Was it overemphasis on the part of Saint Bridgid when she declared that it had been made known to her that all Hell trembles at the very mention of Mary's name?

It is a very great pity that there is not more place in Catholic studies not only for Mariology in general, but for the simple devotions to Our Lady.

Moreover, if it is true . . . and it probably is true . . . that *most* educated Catholics are well-informed on Marian devotion, the thing to be deplored is that they had to inform themselves; and if the material

for this self-information had not been at hand, they
might have gone forth from college or seminary and
through their entire lives without being able to
answer some fundamental Catholic questions, and
without being able to take the hands of the less educated and place them in Our Lady's hand for sheer
ignorance of where Our Lady's hand might best be
found.

This complaint is not new. And we can thank
Heaven that it is growing to the point where something may be done about it. Certainly the meaning and necessity of devotion to Our Lady has
doubled its emphasis during recent years.

I do not know whether I speak from a unique experience. But I do speak from experience . . . a
fairly well-crossed experience . . . that has at times
been bitter.

However, appearing thus in this book . . . obviously a deliberate diversion from the general context
and discussed at a disproportionately great length,
this criticism of Catholic attitude in America towards Our Lady and Her primary devotions will
seem much more severe than is intended.

Most Catholic priests, and *most* Catholics, have a
very deep and a very tender devotion to Our Lady.
And this was never more evident than in war-time,
with the Rosary prayed fervently for Victory, various Novenas to Our Lady attended in great number,
thousands making all sorts of sacrifices to clothe

Service men in Mary's Scapular, and with Catholic chaplains, the world over, preaching devotion to Mary in camp and trench.

This complaint is addressed at *education*. For of what avail is it that the Church transmits a mighty devotion for centuries, enriching it unspeakably almost in competition with the miraculous riches heaped upon it from Heaven, if this same devotion is not *explained* to the generations now to come, and if its relation to the Mass and the Sacraments is not understood?

Perhaps the point to be made is that plain faith . . . through tradition and her allies . . . is no longer sufficient.   Scientific skepticism has created a certain amount of religious skepticism. And therefore the fundamental reasons for our devotions should be taught as well as the facts.   There are *reasons* why we should be devoted to Mary, and there are *reasons* why *certain devotions* to Mary are excellent in themselves and perhaps more excellent than others. And educators should know these reasons, so that they will themselves be able to give a rational explanation.   And that is why criticism is leveled particularly at the seminary curriculum and the usual college course in Religion, because these curricula too much overlook the science of Marian devotions . . . which devotions certainly are not non-essential. "If the world would but turn to devotion to Mary," said Pope Pius IX, "it would speedily be saved."

CHAPTER EIGHTEEN

Back to Carmel

WHILE I was at Saint Leo's Abbey, a new possibility had presented itself: the foreign service. It happens that a friend of the family was a Consul in one of our large cities, and this Consul (at least until war was declared) had much time to himself, and yet was handsomely paid. So it occurred to me that I would have ample time to write, until the Scapular Press came of age, if I got myself a similar job.

I wrote to a friend in Congress and asked him to do what he could, and in a few days I received a sheaf of literature from the Department of State.

Upon reading the literature, I found that most of it was signed: G. Howland Shaw, Undersecretary of State. I thought for a moment. Wasn't that name familiar to me? Did I not have a letter . . . ? And then I suddenly realized that this Undersecretary of State, in charge of the personnel of the diplomatic service, had sent me a letter congratulating me on *Mary in Her Scapular Promise,* which he had read and very much admired!

On my way North, therefore, feeling that this per-

haps was the way Our Lady intended to take care of
me for the writing of books, I "dropped in" at the
Department of State in Washington. Mr. Shaw was
busy, but would see me at noon. So I stopped over
at a neighboring museum and passed the interven-
ing hour.

Mr. Shaw took his responsibility too seriously, of
course, to give a high position to someone who would
regard it as an avocation. "A few years ago," he said,
"you might have found a Consul's job, perhaps somewhere in South America, the thing you're looking
for; but with present world conditions you have to
work at it ten hours a day. We need good men
desperately."

Since it was Mr. Shaw's position to direct men in
their vocations, I sought his advice, and in the course
of an hour not only was a friendship formed, but I
got many practical ideas.

My next call that same afternoon (not counting
the call at a police station to pay a fine for passing
through a stop-sign which, preoccupied with my recent visit, I did not see) was to a priest who had
been one of my teachers in the seminary some ten
years before, and who had recently been in Rome as
Assistant General of the Carmelite Order. The
war had forced the Prior General and his American
Assistant to leave Rome and to take up their resi-
dence in the United States, where communication

with the Carmelite Order in most other parts of the world was far more facile.

As was mentioned earlier, *Mary in Her Scapular Promise* had become a best-seller. One of its greatest advocates and admirers was this very priest: the Very Reverend Gabriel N. Pausback, O. Carm.; and he had asked me to stop in to see him.

This was to be my first contact, as a layman, with associates I had known in the seminary. Several of my former classmates had been ordained and were stationed in this house. Before I had joined the Order, I had spent a few weeks at this same house one summer, visiting my uncle who then was Prior there. So when I parked the journey-stained little Ford at the door and walked up the path, I had many mixed feelings.

One of the first persons I met was a priest who had been my best friend and idol, in eight years together at the same classes and at the same table; he was formerly the boy with whom I had skated and played tennis and walked by the hour and made all sorts of friendship pacts. Neither of us could talk. There seemed to be some barrier between us, and yet our eyes told what was in our hearts. "Hi ya, Matt," he said. "Hello, Fa . . Father," I replied, stumbling on the word.

I had never really left the Order, and it had not left me. I had loved it too much for that. It was simply a case of God's Will. I had been chosen to work elsewhere.

Father Pausback received me with great kindness, and what seemed to be eagerness.

"Look here," he said significantly after the usual exchanges, "what do you think of this?"

The sheet he passed to me had the title "Scapular Militia" above a description of the Scapular Devotion and an appeal to give a Scapular Medal to every Catholic boy in the American Armed Forces.

Having recently meditated on the Scapular Medal, the thing I saw principally was that one item. To my mind, filled as I was with months of study on that one subject, any wholesale emphasis on the Scapular Medal would have been a set-back to the devotion and immediately I thought only of how I might convey such a criticism without seeming critical. Thus the significance of the paper was lost to me. But I was to hear a great deal more about it, and I was to see a great deal more of this fiery and meditative priest.

Father Pausback was a fairly young man, tall and wiry, well-informed and intelligent, and having a thoroughly religious attitude towards everything. He was, to my mind, a real Carmelite. The fact that he was Assistant General of the Order at the age of thirty-five was evidence enough of his virtue and ability.

After a talk together, most of which probably neither of us can remember, we parted company.

But we were destined to be partners . . . the layman and the religious . . . in a mighty enterprise.

Father Gabriel, in white cloak, is seen at the right. The Bishop of Fatima holds the Icon of Kazan on steps of the International Centre of the Blue Army at Fatima. This took place almost thirty years after the events of this chapter. . . when the apostolate begun with Father Gabriel had reached to every corner of the world. . . even to restore to the people of Russia the Icon of their "Liberatrix".

CHAPTER NINETEEN

The Right Door

EVER SINCE the morning when I awoke in the Pullman berth in Atlantic City I had been trying, with the hands of my mind, any door that might be the one through which God wanted me to pass. Never for a moment did I doubt that there was such a door, and my criterion for finding it was: The opportunity to establish a Scapular Apostolate.

Perhaps Our Lady was pleased with these futile efforts. Anyway, I think the reader will discover that, all the while, She had Her own plan that we may briefly trace here in the light of what has happened.

The fact that my father published magazines and owned a sizable printing plant presented greatest food for thought. I wanted a magazine in which to express my ideas and in which I could publish the miracles that were going to be wrought through the Scapular; I wanted to flood the country with leaflets; I wanted to publish books.

But enthusiastic as I was, I realized that my father was right in saying that a magazine cannot precede its following, and leaflets distributed by the thousands cost a deal of money, and to publish many books without knowing whether there would be a market was business suicide.

It gradually dawned on me that I would probably have to "go into business" for Our Lady . . . much though business was distasteful to such a born dreamer as myself. So I began to evolve a plan, the basis of which was the "Scapular Press."

First, I laid plans for a Marian magazine, studying editorial technique, typography, make-up, subscription-drives, departments . . . and, by repeated questions, fairly ruining my father's good humor. I wanted to call it "The Scapular," but I thought that title would be premature. So I called it *Through Mary,* and I asked the Carmelites, the Marianists, the Missionary Catechists, and Blessed Grignon de Montfort's Society if they would like to collaborate on this strictly Marian periodical, in which I would forward their own Orders. (The Carmelites and the Society of Blessed Grignon were interested and it looked as though the plan would work. My "scheme," of course, was to emphasize the Scapular in this Marian periodical . . . and thus "by indirection, find direction out.")

Second, I wondered what could be done about the inactivity of the vast Scapular Confraternity . . . a Society in which millions of Catholics became special children of Our Lady of the Scapular and even received Assurance of Salvation from Her, but also a Society in which these Catholics did nothing in return. And I drew up a plan which, worked out in detail, was several pages long and, if I do say so, quite convincing. The plan was described in a letter to the Prior General of the Carmelite Order, asking him to name me President of an American Scapular Society and to give me power to appoint officers in the Confraternity in America who might become apostles for Our Lady in their own locale.

That letter was never mailed .

I had just finished it, and had it piled with sheafs of data on the magazine project for further and final consideration after a few nights of sleep, when I was called to the telephone by the long-distance operator.

The call was from the Assistant General of the Carmelites, in New York City, who wanted to find out whether my services were available, because his Order was interested in founding a Scapular Society, to give Scapulars to boys in the Service, and he thought I might like to cooperate in the job! The immediate sponsors of the project were the Carmelite Fathers of the New York Province, under the zealous leadership of the Very Reverend Lawrence D. Flanagan, O. Carm., and with the expressed wish of the Most Reverend Hilary M. Doswald, Prior General of the Carmelite Order.

It was eight months before Pearl Harbor.

And by that fateful December 8th, when America went into war, I found myself in a bustling office in New York, with the beginning of a magazine called *"The Scapular"* and seven thousand members in an active Scapular Society called "The Scapular Militia."

This, then, was the door.

All the struggles I had made merely prepared me to pass through it when it was opened by Our Lady Herself.

It is not presumptuous to say that the growth of the Scapular Militia was miraculous. Father Pausback worked right along with the organization, in the capacity of Religious Director.

In a short time it mushroomed throughout the nation and soon had Units in almost every large city, from coast to coast.

The Prior General of the Carmelite Order himself, who was exiled in this country by the war, and who had collaborated in the foundation of the Militia, as was mentioned above, wrote the following report when the organization had just finished its *first* year.

"Material has been distributed to Catholic women for 530,000 Scapulars, and already 325,000 completed Scapulars have been returned to the Militia

Headquarters. The chaplains in turn have received 130,000 Scapular packets. The Militia now numbers 6,400 formal members, though persons actively cooperating in the work exceed 10,000. Numerous Marian sodalities, units of the Catholic Daughters of America, and Girl Scout Troops have taken part in the extensive sewing campaign conducted by the Militia. Due to the work of the Militia, the Scapular Medal has become part of the N. C. C. S. kit distributed to our Catholic soldiers. Over one hundred Catholic Colleges and High Schools have contributed to the campaign to raise funds for the enterprise.

"While primarily intended for the spiritual benefit of soldiers, the Scapular Militia has been instrumental in bringing about an increased interest in the Scapular on the part of priests and lay people also. Since December, 1924, one of our American Provincials had received applications for Scapular faculties from only eight priests. Since June of last year he has given faculties to 413 priests, and 507 listed chaplains. The activities of the Militia, as reported in many Catholic newspapers and magazines, has given widespread knowledge of the Scapular, its meaning and efficacy. Approximately 100,-000 pieces of Scapular literature have been distributed. A number of practical Scapular problems have been given public discussion, and their solution put under way. A strenuous campaign has been conducted against the selling of invalid Scapulars. A permanent Scapular Bureau has been established which handles articles of Scapular devotion, and in every way strives to promote Scapular information."

The Prior General made this report in a circular letter to members of the Carmelite Order. When he had finished the above quotations, he added:

"I have presented these results of the Scapular Militia to you because I know that you will, as true Brothers of Our Lady of Mount Carmel, rejoice in the honor She is receiving. While we must felicitate those responsible for its organization and efficient administration, we should regard the Militia as the work and concern not only of a few, but rather as an expression of that inner urge in the Order itself to honor Mary: 'Ratio Ordinis nostri in eo ponenda est quod . . . specialem erga Beatam Virginem Mariam . . . devotionem . . . ubique terrarum praesertim per sacrum Scapulare propagare conetur.' The Carmelite Order is never lacking in devoted sons to spread Our Lady's glory. This work, therefore, as an expression of the living urge of the Order to propagate the Scapular, deserves the active interest and cooperation of all of Carmel's sons."

No one can say where this general Scapular movement that began with a holy lay Brother's "vision" will end. The very consideration of *one million* leaflets completely explaining the Scapular Devotion having been distributed to men in the Service alone is bound to have far-reaching consequences. Above all, we may consider the fact that the book, which has proved the groundwork of the entire movement, went into nineteen thousand copies in three years . . . and one case is known of a single copy having been read by eight hundred nuns. It is also to be noted that hundreds of copies are in use at spiritual libraries; and thousands of copies went into religious houses where, according to many reports, it was read to the entire communities.

In conjunction with the apostolate launched through the Militia, the perpetual Scapular Novena was begun at the Militia Shrine, in New York City, and *in less than a year* after the Novena had begun, *more than fifty thousand copies* of the prayers had been distributed, and wonders reported at the National Shrine were already of frequent occurrence.

The main work, however, still remains, and that is why *this* book has been written. And since I have pointedly made this book so conversational . . . albeit, perforce, one-sided . . . I will tell how the book came to be and what the "Scapular Apostolate" means when put into practice.

I had yet to learn about Our Lady of Fatima.

CHAPTER TWENTY

Why a Layman?

THE SCAPULAR Militia had been organized for four months. I was home for the weekend.

Even an imaginative artist could not have chosen a more ideal spot for what happened. And how well I remember every detail!

It was a log cabin on a wood-bound lake . . . a summer night . . . moonlight vied with a million stars . . . a yellow arc of light flooded the green foliage over the cabin chimney where, inside, over a crackling fire, there sizzled a dozen steaks.

Only six couples were invited. The cabin was privately owned, on an immense, wooded estate. My brother was giving the party . . . otherwise I know I should never have been invited: I did not know how to dance, was stopped at the second drink, and invariably led the conversation around to something religious or academic . . . But my brother insisted that I come, and all that I had to bring was my presence, and a couple of extra frying pans from a boat he had given me.

It was about dusk when I drove up the dirt road,

through beautiful woodland with pine and holly and oak and stopped at the isolated little cabin, for the sake of which God seemed to have planted all the trees and to have laid out the gorgeous square mile of lake that rippled peacefully to the front door.

I was wearing boating clothes, with a comfortable jacket, and was smoking my evening pipe. I had a conscious appetite. The day had started with a "stag" boating trip that was supposed to be for fishing, but which ended in heavy swimming and a succession of such bad luck at the fishing spots that I had practically spent the day pulling a fifty-pound anchor.

Of course, I could make this long story short, but this evening proved to be one of the most momentous of my whole life.

I was one of the first to arrive at the cabin. The colored man who had charge of preparing and serving food and drink was the only one before me.

The cabin had two tremendous rooms, each with a long, stolid dining table, hunting trophies on the walls, fireplace, all sorts of manly gadgets and mementos. In the corner of the larger room was a dusty upright piano, almost adjacent to the fireplace. A stuffed pheasant and a stuffed owl stared down at me.

I cannot remember exactly when she came in. It seems that the whole crowd straggled in almost together. She says I was bending over the fire, tossing a log.

She wasn't supposed to be my "date" anyway.

But a year later, she was the girl I married.

The cabin, the moonlight, the woodland and lake, the mystery of a summer night, were enough to stir romance even in my book-bound soul. But they only contributed. As my father said, when I asked his advice before marriage: "If you looked the world over, you would not find a finer girl."

It wasn't love "at first sight," at least on my side. But the railroad company did a wonderful business between New York and Philadelphia (where she owned a juvenile outfitter's shop) during the following year.

We were supposed to be married at the National Shrine, but it would not do for anyone to marry us but Father John, and he had not been well of late and could not travel. We therefore went to Middletown . . . the city where *Mary in Her Scapular Promise* was written and where, strange to say, the pastor of the church in which the ceremony was performed had so much admired *the symbol of the Scapular Press* that he had had it enlarged and inlaid on the floor before a shrine of Our Lady of the Scapular.

Until the last minute, I was deeply worried about my decision to marry; I was not certain that the marital state would be conducive to the good of my

work.   I had asked God that His Will be done, and
hoped that He would make it known to me.   Then
a little thing happened, shortly before the marriage
that means little itself but which brought me peace.

Whenever I have written anything . . . and it
seems that I spend most of my waking hours writing something or other . . . I always make a little
cross at the top of the sheet and write "Maria!" as
I recite: "In the name of the Father Who created
me, and of the Son Who redeemed me, and of the
Holy Ghost Who sanctifies me, I offer up this action
which I am about to perform, through Mary!"

My fiancée had noticed this sign on all my letters
to her, and when she gave instructions to have the
wedding ring engraved she told the jeweler to use
this sign . . . the cross over the word "Maria!" . . .
and then to write after that "To A. E. K. from J.
M. H." And she did not have the slightest idea of
the personal consecration which the sign implied.

When I saw the engraving, it seemed almost as
though I were seeing a Heavenly consecration of the
contract I was "now about to perform."

The marriage ceremony was beautiful.   I had
been working in the office until a half-hour before
train-time, and I had no thought of ordering flowers or in any way preparing for the ceremony.   But
when I entered the church the next morning, the
entire sanctuary was overflowing with gladioli and
roses, and a choir of Carmelite theologians from the

seminary, beautifully trained, were singing a hymn to Our Lady.

It was the first time in his many years as priest, as he had never been a pastor, that Father John had ever been called upon to say a nuptial Mass. Father Pausback had traveled all the way from Chicago, and was kneeling in the sanctuary with the venerable Father Provincial . . . the Very Reverend Lawrence D. Flanagan, O. Carm. . . . who had come from New York. It was a solemn-high Mass, with two other Carmelite priests assisting at the altar.

The beauty of the nuptial ceremony is beyond words. Attended in proper spirit, the Nuptial Mass seems to bring a stream of graces into the soul of man and woman that transform them for that unselfish partnership . . . in which they share all that they are and all that they have, ceasing at that moment to be independent.

Before marriage I had been nervous, often fighting a sense of irritation, distracted by worry of where and what to eat and of the cleanliness of my house and of the order of my clothing. Above all, I had never really known the meaning of self-abnegation for another, which is true fraternal charity. I understand now why there is such a warm attitude about conscientious married folk. This was an innuendo of human character I had never before noticed, and which even yet I could not define.

I could not help drawing a comparison between this new state and my former state.

In some respects there is an entirely different mentality between the cleric and the layman. The natural drives in a religious can never include personal economic aggrandizement; and this drive is usually a necessity in the layman's makeup, and it increases the layman's sense of dependence on God. On the other hand, of course, the religious is not distracted by worldly cares and attachments, and can thus devote full creative energy to his work.

I had only been married a short time when Father Pausback started a drive at the National Shrine to increase its chapter of the Third Order Carmelite.

"Have you ever joined the Third Order?" he asked me one morning.

"I have thought about it for the past five years, Father," I answered, "but every time I had the opportunity to join I knew I wasn't good enough, and I postponed."

"The Third Order is supposed to make you better, John," Father replied. "It would be foolish to postpone exercise to make yourself stronger because you don't feel strong enough to take it."

So, after such long hesitation, I joined, and I asked my bride whether she would like to join with me. When she learned what the Third Order was, she became as eager to join as I was myself.

Three days before the ceremony of investiture in

the Third Order Habit, Father Pausback came straight to my office in the morning.

"The Director of the Third Order is pleased to know that you are going to join, John," he said, "and he invites you to address the Third Order chapter, in the church, after the ceremony."

This would be the first time I had ever spoken to a congregation before the Blessed Sacrament! By marriage, I had closed the door on my longing to be a priest to forever join the ranks of laity from which the vast membership of the Scapular Apostolate must come. And now I was to have an unexpected priestly privilege.

The talk I gave made me choke with feeling, and the congregation did a little choking, too. Everyone knew I had recently married, since the banns had been published in that parish, so I admitted that I had not felt worthy to join the Third Order for several years and that, by providential coincidence, I was joining shortly after I had married.

"It is for the First and Second Orders to pray and work, and it is for us, the laity, to raise families in the Spirit of Christ. And by joining the Third Order with my wife, I feel as though both of us had taken the hand of Our Lady in starting out into life together with one heart, one mind, one soul to achieve God's Will for others, and our mutual salvation."

The "right door" had closed behind me.

CHAPTER TWENTY-ONE

Miracles?

PUBLIC RECOGNITION of the Scapular Militia began when the Most Reverend John F. O'Hara, Bishop of the American Armed Forces, blessed ten thousand Scapulars in Our Lady's chapel of Saint Patrick's Cathedral, with the Prior General of the Carmelites present. Pictures of the scene appeared in Catholic papers all over the country.

One news-release followed another, each one containing the name and address of the National Shrine.

But only a handful of people joined the organization!

After *three months,* we had less than one hundred members, and we had invested over two thousand dollars (albeit of credit) in the printing of folders, in the buying of office equipment, materials for making Scapulars, and other necessities.

It was nearing the Feast of Our Lady of the Scapular, which falls on July 16th, and elaborate plans had been made to celebrate the Feast at the church which the office adjoined . . . the Church of Our Lady of the Scapular of Mount Carmel. With the aid of a part-time secretary I constituted the office force . . . writer, business director, shipping and filing clerk . . . and we "all" intended to recreate on the Feast Day, especially since the mail brought only two and three letters a day to keep us busy.

It was taking a pretty strong vote of confidence in Our Lady of the Scapular to face the future with optimism, after a stream of publicity for three months had brought such negligible results.

However, on the Vigil of the Feast, *over one hundred letters came in the morning mail alone!* Within the week after the feast, the membership of the Militia jumped to almost one thousand.

Soon the little office adjoining the church was too small; so we moved most of the material to the second floor of the parish school and kept the church office as the reception office. Gradually an office force was hired and, almost miraculously, six large desks appeared in one room, shelves went up in another room, and from almost nowhere came working tables and chairs and filing cases and other requisite equipment.

Particularly memorable is the first filing cabinet. I had just remarked to my secretary, before going to lunch: "If only we had a place to file all those letters!" And when I came back there were six brand new filing drawers in the office, anonymously donated!

At first, all the desks were in one large room, and

it was bedlam. Four typewriters were going at once, and visitors kept coming and going constantly. I was gradually becoming a nervous case.

One morning had been particularly difficult and I went out to lunch choking with chagrin. "It's impossible to do creative work in that office!" I moaned to myself. "If only I had a private office somewhere! By George, I'm going to see about getting one if it puts us *twice* as badly into debt!" And I came back to work feeling no better than I had felt when I left, even though I had stopped in at the Shrine to ask Our Lady's prayers.

When I walked down the corridor towards the main office, to my astonishment I saw the door of a room that had always been closed off standing wide, and the room was piled high with office equipment!

In the time that I was gone, a truck had arrived bringing complete office equipment . . . filing cases, two desks, chairs, tables . . . even the supply of ink and rubber bands and the decorative plant.

All of this equipment was an unheralded donation from an organization closed by the war.

The next day, needless to say, I was working in a private office.

And these wonders that we experienced at the National Shrine were being experienced also by the people working for the Militia.

A woman in Buffalo who had suffered for years with acute rheumatism was seen walking the streets in mid-winter. When asked for an explanation of this wonder, she said: "I was making Scapulars, and my rheumatism left me."

In California, a woman had prayed for a certain favor for years . . . having offered up various novenas and having had many Masses said. On the Vigil of All-Saints Day, she was making Scapulars for the Militia and the thought came: "Why not ask Our Lady of the Scapular to help you?" Immediately she said: "Dear Virgin, if I obtain this favor I will donate a thousand dollars to the Militia."

On All-Souls Day, itself, the favor was granted. In the next mail, a check for one thousand dollars went to the National Shrine . . . where it was received as another miracle, because we had been urgently praying for funds!

After the Scapular Novena was started, wonders became a regular occurrence.

Although not directly connected with the Militia, there are two wonders that greatly affected me.

During this time, while Father John was visiting his sister, in Pleasantville, New Jersey, I remember that a woman suffering with a badly infected leg came from a farm some miles distant, at great inconvenience, believing that if Father John would touch his stole to her leg it would be instantly cured. I was there at the time, and I shall never forget the deep faith expressed by that afflicted soul; if ever faith was strong enough to move mountains, I thought to myself, it was like this.

Father John applied the stole but, despite the woman's faith, nothing happened.

Later, a specialist had been called and he decided that the infection had so spread that science could do no more; that the leg would have to be amputated. Father John wrote to the woman and told her to put the Scapular on her leg and ask Our Lady of the Scapular to heal it.

When the doctor came the next day, the amputation was unnecessary. At the precise moment that the woman touched the Scapular to her leg the pain left, and she completely recovered.

Father John had a similar experience with his own mother. She became paralyzed, and a Protestant doctor said that nothing could cure her because of the severity of the stroke and her advanced age. Father John said: "There is absolutely no hope?" "If she walked again," the doctor said significantly, "it would be a miracle."

Father John fastened a pair of Scapulars on his mother's legs.

She grew steadily better and regained complete use of her legs.

With these, and particularly the other *very extraordinary* favors continually being wrought, but for which we have not the space, I almost apologize for closing this chapter with the little story I am about to tell, but I do so because it bears directly upon the Scapular Apostolate.

When the Novena was being launched, I very much wanted it to close with the singing of the brief hymn that Saint Simon Stock was saying when Our Lady gave him the Scapular. But there was no music to the approved English translation. It was the week before the Novena opened and I awoke during the night and decided to write a simple melody myself.

I had once before composed a "Flos Carmeli" to the Latin words, and someone who knew the laws of composition found a great many flaws in it. So I did not want to risk the harmonization of this new melody, simple though it was, and I wondered who might do it. In all New York, I did not at once know where to turn.

The next day, through a mutual acquaintance I came to meet the piano accompanist of Giovanni Martinelli, Doctor Emilo Roxas ... who had written a book on harmony and who had been assistant-conductor to Mascagni, in Lyons, France. I gave him a copy of *Mary in Her Scapular Promise,* and the following day he telephoned to the National Shrine, wondering if there was something, anything he could do, with his knowledge of music, to help.

The day before the novena opened the little hymn was ready, and it had been harmonized by one of the world's great masters. A year later it was heard in a radio broadcast throughout the nation, sung by the famous Jessica Dragonette, just several hours after she received an award as America's outstanding concert radio singer.

Our Lady does not do even the slightest things by halves!

Our daughter took this picture of myself and my wife at a dinner in 1970. The years do not seem to have taken much of a toll although twenty-eight years had passed since we took each other "for better or for worse".

CHAPTER TWENTY-TWO

Groundwork

IT WOULD not be far wrong for me to convey the impression that the Scapular Apostolate just dropped from Heaven . . . membership, shrine, magazine, organization, novena, public relations, and all.

The founding of the Apostolate was fraught with but few problems. The Militia was supposed to be a war-time project, to give Scapulars to Service men. But it almost automatically proved to be not only a war-time project but also the opening of a door towards which, in painful darkness, the trust from Brother had been leading.

While working towards the ultimate goal of a Scapular Apostolate . . . which our country had always needed but which it took a war to uncover . . . I was interested primarily in helping with the task of getting Scapulars to the boys in the Service, not only because that was the publicized object of the "Scapular Militia" but also because it was one of the best possible objects of a Scapular Apostolate and I found that the Carmelite Fathers had already been planning for the same goal.

In accomplishing this primary objective for Service men (who needed the Scapular) the Militia staff was anxious to establish an Apostolate that would never die.

In the years of waiting and of expectancy, I had made many plans. There was to be organization . . . with local units spread throughout the country, led by holy men and women in love with Our Lady and anxious to use Her "Promise of Salvation" to help insure the salvation of souls. There was to be a special magazine to knit the organization together and to be a clearing-house for progressive thought and an editorial fire at which the hearts of all members might be enflamed with zeal and love. There was to be prayer: perpetual novena, and the Morning offering. There was to be a National Shrine, under the altar of which the names of all members would be placed to be remembered in special votive Masses of Our Lady of the Scapular.

But I did not have to make any effort whatsoever to realize these plans. They were all *demanded by the war-time project itself.*

First, organization was imperative. The Scapulars had to be made for the Service men and that meant promoters and sewing circles; some sort of reward had to be made to stimulate a holy competition in the organization, and that gave rise to from one to twenty-five years of membership in the organization for donations made or work accomplished, with special Mass remembrances as the reward for each year of membership; and the communication system throughout the membership . . . which soon became so large that mimeographed bulletins were as expensive as printed ones . . . within *two years* demanded, of necessity, a magazine which has not yet had enough pages to contain all that it fairly bursts to say; the novena and offering were demanded by the members themselves, who soon began to ask whether there wasn't some weekly devotion or some prayers to be said in honor of Our Lady of the Scapular, because they wanted to pray.

And that is why it seems as though the whole program, *in full act,* had suddenly dropped from Heaven. One year it was a blind street, and the very next year it was a busy highway.

Most members of the Militia had never thought of the apostolic possibilities of the Scapular Promises. Naturally, when they heard the appeal to help assure the salvation of boys facing death on battlefields, they instinctively thought of a similar appeal for an aged relative, or a sick friend; some thought of all aged people, everywhere; some thought of the domestic and foreign missions; most thought of anyone near and dear to them whose salvation might be in any doubt.

Thus the mail brought many, many suggestions, and appeals, to continue the Apostolate after the war.

Of course, even before the Militia was organized, Father Pausback recognized the providential character of the Apostolate. Particularly after learning the story told in this book his efforts became ceaseless. He knew no rest. Almost his every waking thought, in so far as official priestly and Curial business would permit, was for the progress of the Scapular Apostolate. In July, 1943, in celebration of the Scapular Feast, not only did his voice reach millions in a coast-to-coast broadcast on the Scapular Devotion, but he organized, at the National Shrine, an immense religious-patriotic parade and demonstration that might have been the envy of any country in which Our Lady's Scapular Promises have been ceaselessly recognized and honored for centuries. And this was by way of precedent.

In May of this same year, the Prior General of the Order, the Most Reverend Hilary Maria Doswald, issued a pastoral which commanded and specified unity on all disputed Scapular questions, and which officially assured the progress of the Scapular Apostolate by ordaining *special classes* for the study of the Scapular Devotion in the Carmelite seminaries. This was perhaps one of the most significant acts of a Carmelite Prior General, for the furtherance of the Scapular Devotion, since the thirteenth century.

After the appearance of *Mary in Her Scapular Promise* (November, 1940), in which a special appeal was made for writing and preaching about the

Scapular, many magazine articles appeared on the subject. One of the best was by Father William A. Donaghy, S. J., Associate Editor of *America,* and it led to a personal friendship between myself and this wonderful Jesuit that ultimately gave birth to this present book, which he encouraged me to write despite my own misgivings.

However, it is not my purpose to give credit in this chapter to the various leaders in the Apostolate . . . from the Carmelite Order, from other members of the clergy, and from the laity . . . because that would not be possible. There are easily a hundred active leaders, at the time of this writing, who have *as much or more right than myself* to be in this little history. And their number increases steadily.

The branches of the Scapular Apostolate's organization can best be summarized by the simple star that has for centuries been a symbol associated with Our Lady of the Scapular.

The two supporting points of the star are commerce and donations; the two central points are formal organization (Units) and communication (especially by the magazine); the peak point is charity (giving scapulars, with explanatory literature, where most needed) and the apostolate of prayer (which includes novenas for favors sought, but eminently implies the highest point of the apostolate: living the morning offering).

It can be said that this star did drop from Heaven in that it has appeared almost miracuously here on earth. And Our Blessed Lady is choosing leaders for the Apostolate, to help accomplish Her mission of "Uniting all mankind in Christ" by means of Her greatest of all promises . . . the promise of eternal salvation.

Some of these leaders have been making positively staggering physical and financial sacrifices.

This activity, which has been reminding so many American Catholics of the significance of the Scapular Devotion, is the groundwork and container of an even more significant apostolate: The apostolate of the extended Morning Offering . . . of all "For Jesus through Mary."

Beyond my most remote expectations, this was to be accomplished through the whole world with the establishment of an International Centre in Fatima, Portugal, and with the special and direct intervention of the Holy Father himself.

CHAPTER TWENTY-THREE

From Their Fruits

THE READER will notice that I have alluded to *Mary in Her Scapular Promise* as the intellectual *groundwork* for the wordless apostolate . . . the apostolate to draw souls to Jesus, through Mary, even without words.

Mary in Her Scapular Promise does not treat of any organized apostolate. It merely demonstrates that a tremendous *power is latent in the Scapular Confraternity,* and it suggests that wonderful things would happen in this world were all wearers of the Scapular to recognize this hidden power, and to utilize it.

The appeal to a specific apostolate, with the "Morning Offering," was to be a book which I have decided not to write, I decided, instead, simply to tell what happened, leaving the appeal for apostles in Our Lady's hands.

The strongest appeal is the appeal based on facts, just as the strongest argument is the argument of facts. Our Lord pointed this out when He said: "By their fruits ye shall know them."

The facts are these.

A lay-brother, whom I knew to be of unusual purity of soul and nearness to God, as I have described to the reader, had what seemed to be a private revelation. When he left for Palestine, hoping for martyrdom, he said simply: "If it is to be, God will see to it."

Therefore, could I offer any better argument for the message which Brother entrusted to me?

The reader will recall that I at once made known, on beginning the book, that I am not a mystic, but a comfortable "businessman." Then the reader was carried back through the extraordinary experience of meeting a saintly Brother.

Then came the dénouement.

We accused this Brother of having an apparition, and we drew from him the extraordinary statement that closes the sixth chapter: "This message was saved until now, placed before me, and taken by you to be made known to the world."

After that, everything went contrary to expectation. When we expected approval from the confessor most likely to believe, we had to burn every scrap of evidence. (Now, however, is an acceptable time to admit that Father John kept the copy that had been sent to him, and later returned it.) Then came separation; the world was literally placed between the one who said "My duty is to pray," and between the one of whom he said: "It is for you to write and to do the work."

Unexpectedly, almost inexplicably, the latter returned from the Carmelite Order to the world . . . having been in the Order just long enough to receive the message and to study it.

From that time forward, the things that happened to me, as I wandered from one door to another seeking a door that would lead to a fulfillment of my "trust," were forcing out the cry: *Is* there a *right* door?"

I was so convinced that there was a right door that I refused to publish a book after working on it for weeks on end and began, as the reader remembers, an almost nomadic existence, with absolutely no assurance of victory and . . . at first . . . no one, including those closest and dearest, to believe with me.

Then things began to happen. The sister of Saint Therese, whom the Saint had called "My little Mother," placed the realization of the work in the hands of her sainted sister. Monsignor Sheen wrote the preface to the book *Mary in Her Scapular Promise*. Opposition to the founding of the Scapular

Press crumbled with the wonderful origin of a symbol, appearing where lines had been scribbled. Lectures "caught on." And finally a real apostolate was launched, with the Carmelite Fathers establishing a National Shrine, a foundation of Masses for members of the Apostolate, and so on.

These, then, are the facts.

Another door was to open... This is an unusual and heretofore unpublished picture of the author with Msgr. Harold Colgan who was to turn a "March of Pledges" into an Army for the Queen...

CHAPTER TWENTY-FOUR

Four Pillars

WITH THE Scapular, Our Lady has lowered a bridge to our hearts across the chasm of the world. "Whosoever dies clothed in this," She proclaims, "shall not suffer eternal fire."

To the casual observer, this bridge seems flimsy. But to the careful observer, this bridge is seen to stand on four inflexible pillars . . . the pillars of *homage, confidence, love and alliance*.

For centuries . . . *before* the Scapular Bridge was lowered . . . the Catholic Church believed that anyone who perseveringly practiced a devotion of homage, of confidence, and of love towards Mary *could not be lost*. Those three elements of devotion constitute *true* devotion, and the Doctors of the Church were unanimous in proclaiming that a true devotee of the Immaculate Virgin (over whom Satan had never had dominion) could not be lost.

When She gave the Scapular, Our Lady instituted a sign of alliance, the use of which constitutes a true devotion to Her . . . a devotion of homage, confidence and love.

Anyone who wears the Scapular has a mutual contract with Our Lady: She has promised to save; he pledges, as a member of Her Carmelite family on earth, to wear Her sign. This is a true alliance.

One who wears the Scapular desires to have Mary as his Mother; he wears the Scapular because he wants Mary's help and protection. And this desire is love.

One who wears the Scapular wears a sign that denotes reverence for Mary: and this is homage.

Finally, one who wears the Scapular does so because he believes in Mary's promises and power. And this is confidence.

But is it enough to have a bridge between ourselves and the Immaculate Heart of Mary? Above all, is it wise for us to refuse to *cross this bridge?*

Millions of Catholics wear the Scapular and never advert to its ascetical value. They remember simply that it is richly indulgenced and privileged. And thus they ignore *why* it is indulgenced and privileged, and lose its essential value . . . value that is beyond human understanding, because it is the value of MARY.

This "bridge-crossing" is called an *apostolate* for two reasons: It leads to self-perfection; and it enables Our Lady to release the torrent of Grace that is enclosed in Her Immaculate Heart, awaiting our prayer for its release.

All this is explained fully in *Mary in Her Scapular Promise,* particularly in the last chapter. Here we wish to answer the question: "How shall I practice this apostolate?"

A.   As an apostolate of *self-perfection and prayer,* a person may do the following two things:

1)   Say the Morning Offering (mentioned earlier in this book) every day.

2)   Frequently during the day (perhaps when the clock strikes, or when occupation is changed) *remember* that by the Scapular you are *allied* to Mary, and rededicate yourself and your actions to Her disposition.

(It is also urgently recommended, albeit in poor taste, that the latter chapters of *Mary in Her Scapular Promise* be *read and re-read,* so that the importance and meaning of the above two practices may be ever more fully realized.)

B.   As an *apostolate of action,* over and above the two practices already mentioned, one might add the following:

1)   Consider the Promise of Salvation, which Our

Lady attached to the Scapular, as a weapon for conquering souls. Your motto will be: "To anyone whom I cause to wear the Scapular until death, I assure eternal salvation!". And with this goal, *interest others in wearing the Scapular* by disseminating literature, by talking about the Scapular, by distributing Scapulars.

2)   *Preach the Apostolate of Scapular prayer,* mentioned above. It is practically the same as the Apostleship of Prayer, being little more than a spreading of the morning offering throughout the day by a deepening of the alliance achieved by Our Lady with the Scapular. *The strength of this apostolate will depend on the number practicing it.*

Let us consider how a Mr. and a Mrs. Jones, and a Father Reilly and a Sister Maria, and a Lay-Brother Francis, would go about the fulfillment of the Scapular Apostolate.

Father John and the Brother before outdoor statue of Our Lady of Monnt Carmel.

CHAPTER TWENTY-FIVE

Practice

MR. JONES does not go to Mass every day; he feels that attending Mass on Sunday is enough. He goes to Confession about every other month, because he never has very much to confess. Besides, he usually goes to a late Mass and doesn't get to Communion unless it's Holy Name Sunday.

The Scapular Apostolate is designed for just such a man as Mr. Jones.

"It doesn't take much energy to offer up the works of your day while kissing your Scapular in the morning, does it Mr. Jones?" his conscience may ask him. "No, I guess not," he is forced to answer. "And you are *not* doing as much as you should do in the way of prayer, are you, Mr. Jones?" And he is again forced to answer "No." And he thereupon decides that he would like to sanctify the good, and at least the indifferent actions of his day, through Mary, by the good intention.

If Mr. Jones is faithful to that little practice *of adverting to his alliance with Mary* . . . an alliance that bears Her promise that he will one day be in

138

Heaven, and if he is faithful *to the offering of what
he does* . . . through Mary . . . for the intentions of
the Sacred Heart, he will see a wonderful transfor-
mation occur within himself. His life will acquire a
new meaning. He will discover greater imperfection
in himself and will want to go to Confession more
often. Above all, Mr. Jones will come *to think more
of spiritual values* and particularly of the greatest
source of these values: the Holy Eucharist.

At first, Mr. Jones was not at all interested in
getting other people to wear the Scapular . . . and,
least of all, to say the morning offering every day, and
to think of the offering occasionally during the day.
"A man's religion is his own secret," Mr. Jones would
say, "and I'm no preacher."

But seeing in himself the effect of such a simple
thing as true devotion to Mary actively practiced,
Mr. Jones meets his old friend at the Monday night
poker club and thinks to himself: "Poor Joe! He's
missing so much in life! He wouldn't be disturbed
by worries so much if he had his eye a little more on
the next life." And before he is aware of it, Mr.
Jones is saying out of the quiet corner of his mouth:
"Say, Joe, do you wear the Scapular?" And when
Joe is wearing the Scapular, Mr. Jones will be saying: "Did you ever hear of the Apostleship of
Prayer?"

And thus, while he would bristle if someone "accused" him of "preaching," Mr. Jones will have

persuaded Joe to wear the Scapular and offer the actions of his day, through Mary, for the best interests of the Sacred Heart.

Mrs. Jones is in a different category. She may not go to Mass every day, but she does go more often than every Sunday. She thinks Mr. Jones is a "good man," but more than a few times she finds herself praying that he will "get more religion."

The Apostolate of the Scapular was made for Mrs. Jones, too.

Saint Alphonsus tells us of a vision of two ladders, with Our Lord at the top of one ladder and Our Lady at the top of the other: Men trying to climb the ladder to Our Lord were falling back; and those climbing to Our Lady were going up easily. This, Saint Alphonsus explained, was the portrayal of a soul going directly to God without much consideration of Our Lady versus the soul going to Our Lady that it might come, through Her, to God. The first type of soul is climbing the wrong ladder. Our Lord has willed to come down to us through His Mother, and He wills that we climb up to Him in the same manner.

Does Mrs. Jones know this?

"By the Scapular, the Mother of God has laid a bridge to your soul, Mrs. Jones," her conscience may say to her, "and don't you think it would be profitable to cross that bridge? Don't you think it would be wise to think often of the fact that you are allied

to God's Mother? Don't you think you ought to let
God see more of His Immacuate Mother in your
life?"

And as an honest answer, Mrs. Jones consecrates
the actions of her day into the hands of Mary, kissing
her Scapular fondly as an embrace with her Heavenly Mother as she thus surrenders her entire being,
through Mary, into the all-consuming embrace of
the Sacred Heart.

It is not long before Mrs. Jones realizes actively
the wonder of having Mary for a Mother. And despite herself she is soon telling her neighbors about it.

Father Reilly's entire life is devoted to religious
works. He says his morning Mass, his Office, his private prayers; he hears Confessions and visits the
sick; he explains the faith from the pulpit.

The Scapular Apostolate belongs to Father Reilly
in a special way.
"Whatever devotion to Mary can do for Mr. and
Mrs. Jones, as people, it can do for me as a man,"
Father Reilly will say to himself. "And it will do
more for me, because I am pledged to a higher perfection."

But it is particularly the Scapular Apostolate of
action that is Father Reilly's birthright. People need
the Sacraments more, and if it is devotion to Mary

that will bring them the grace of this realization, then it is devotion to Mary that Father Reilly wants his people to practice . . . and particularly the devotion which guarantees, on the word of God's Mother, that those who practice it will not be lost. "Ah," says Father Reilly to himself, "if only I knew that everybody entrusted to me had the Scapular on while dying . . . I could say to the Master: 'Not one of those whom thou didst entrust to me has been lost!' I have the word of Your Mother for it!"

Father Reilly has the advantage of the pulpit. It may not be Mr. Jones' right to preach, but it is Father Reilly's duty. And Father Reilly will see that his people learn about the devotion of the Scapular, and about purifying their actions by consecrating them to Mary that the satisfactions be dispensed in the best interests of the Sacred Heart.

What Father Reilly will need most for his task is knowledge. Almost any book on the Blessed Virgin will help him, because the alpha and omega of the Scapular devotion is alliance with the Blessed Virgin. Perhaps *The Glories of Mary*, by Saint Alphonsus Liguori, and *True Devotion to the Blessed Virgin,* by Blessed Grignon de Montfort, will be of greatest value to him. Books specifically on the Scapular could be obtained from the National Shrine.

Another opening for Father Reilly is the Scapular Novena. The devotion of praying to Our Lady of the Scapular on every Wednesday night dates back many centuries, and there are indulgences to be gained by all the faithful attending the service in a Confraternity church. Father Reilly can send a card or letter to the National Shrine, in New York, requesting personal faculties to enroll in the Scapular and to commute the conditions of the Sabbatine Privilege, and also for the erection of the Confraternity in his church, if it was never erected there before, and from the same source he can obtain any literature or information he needs.

Now we come to Sister Maria.

Sister Maria teaches school. She sometimes wishes she had been a man so that she might have become a priest.

The Scapular Apostolate can bring many blessings, much satisfaction, and much happiness, to Sister Maria.

"Whosoever dies clothed in this Scapular," Our Lady said, "shall not suffer eternal fire!" And Sister Maria works with growing children, amenable souls which can easily be placed beneath that Scapular . . . and thus assured, by Mary's own word, of eternal salvation!

But the joy of assuring the salvation of souls is not all that comes to Sister Maria. Being truly Catholic, Sister feels for the Catholics in other parts of the world who are suffering, she feels for the souls in Purgatory, she feels for the suffering endured by the Church in current persecution. And thus Sister

Maria finds tremendous solace in knowing that all she does, as the child and affiliate of the Immaculate Mother of God, is being sanctified and beautified by the hands of Our Lady as Our Lady applies all to the best interests of the Most Sacred Heart of Jesus. With what fervor Sister Maria makes her morning offering! And how often, with equal fervor, recalling her union with Mary through the Scapular, she renews that offering through the day!

Only in Heaven will we know the number of souls assured of salvation and the world-wide good accomplished by simple, quiet Sister Maria, who taught school.

Of Brother Francis . . . who sweeps corridors and serves at the table . . . who would suspect a great apostle . . . an apostle reaching millions of souls?

Everything that Brother Francis does is done out of the love of God. He is the servant of the servants of God. And how pleasing his actions must be to God as they reach His Heart through the heart of His Immaculate Mother!

"I am allied to Mary by the Scapular, and consecrated to God by my vows," Brother Francis can say, "and all that I do shall be Mary's as so many weapons in Her hands to lay low the enemies of Her Divine Son, and to enlighten the most needy souls with Grace."

The reader need not be told what wonders the

Apostolate of Brother Francis will achieve. Saint Therese of the Child Jesus became Patroness of the Missions because of just such an apostolate.

* * * * *

Every Catholic will find his counterpart in one of the persons described here, or in a mixture of them.

The Scapular bridge was built by Our Lady to be crossed, and to be crossed by all.

The Church sings in the preface of the Mass of Our Lady of the Scapular: ". . . through the holy Scapular, She took to Herself *special* children."

But *all* of the redeemed are Our Lady's children; She has a mother's anxiety for the sanctification and salvation of all. Therefore, what the passage means is: ". . . by the holy Scapular, Our Lady made it possible for us to be more especially Her children . . . made it possible for us to be in a special way morally united to Her, inseparably, unto death."

The choosing is to be made on our side: Will we, or will we not, be special children of Mary? Our Lady offers the Scapular; it is our option to use it or not to use it.

Naturally the reader is left to his own decision about most of the things that have been said in this book. But some of it is just common sense, and the rest is fact.

We are not living in ordinary times, if indeed any times can be called ordinary. We are living in unusually dangerous times. The persecution which Catholics in many parts of the world are now called upon to face is an insidious, poisonous persecution. It is not the persecution of bludgeon and dagger, but the persecution of deadly narcotics concealed in appetising dishes.

The *only* guard against such a deadly persecution is spiritual strength. And spiritual strength does not come solely from Sunday Mass and avoidance of decalogue violations. It comes from inward conviction, and from appreciation and frequentation of the Sacraments.

A way of insuring our approach to this strength is true devotion to Mary.

Our Lady is likened to the neck of the Mystical Body . . . Christ is the Head and we are the trunk. All Grace . . . which is the Life of the Body . . . flows from Christ, through Mary, to us. Where the neck is severed . . . as it was severed by the Reformation . . . the flow of Life splashes away.

A Catholic who lacks true devotion to Mary is not a good Catholic, regardless of his obedience to the Commandments and to the laws of the Church. He is overlooking an essential part of the Divine plan: The Divine plan not only for our redemption but for our sanctification. And when the poison of an ever increasing materialism presses its way into his soul, the soul withers and dies.

One of the things that would amaze anyone coming from the seclusion of a studious life into an active life in the world, would be the number of fallen-away Catholics. Literally tens of thousands of Catholics stop going to church during each succeeding decade. The falling away does not come at once, but gradually.

And is there anyone who can doubt that if these people had practiced a persevering devotion to the Blessed Virgin that they would never have lost their love of spiritual activities? As Saint Alphonsus says, it has *never* been known that a devotee of Mary was lost.

And among devotions to Mary, naturally some are better than others in drawing us to the Sacraments. Of such devotions, Blessed Claude de la Colombière, S. J., coadjutor to Saint Margaret Mary Alacoque in making known the celebrated revelations of the Sacred Heart, said: "The Scapular is the most favored of all." It was given to us specifically as a sign of alliance to Mary, and of assured salvation.

Does it not follow that we need the Scapular today, more than ever before?

Yes, it is not the pieces of cloth and string that we need, any more than we need the paper on which a contract is written, or any more than we need the chalice which holds the Precious Blood. It is the contract itself that we need, and MARY, who comes to us in that contract.

There is no time for delay, and that is why this

present book has been written in a manner almost careless of propriety. Our Lady needs an Army to fight with Her that She may crush the head of the infernal serpent, and we must be that Army. We must clothe ourselves in the Sign of Mary, which assures victory over Hell, and we must unite in an offering of all that we are and have and do that She may apply everything to our own betterment and to the world-wide interests of the Sacred Heart.

We must make the Scapular Apostolate our way of life: To Jesus in the Eucharist, through Mary in the Scapular.

A wonderful path has been laid among skeptics by the Miraculous Medal. Many thousands of non-Catholics, from the famous Ratisbonne down to one of the most recent catechists, have found the miracle of conversion through this simple devotion to Our Lady . . . which professes no other strength than confidence in Her and is even sometimes worn in merely half-skeptical homage. And Our Lady's manifestation of Herself in various parts of the world during recent years, followed by continual miracles now well-known even to agnostic scientists, can be compared to the manifestations of Our Lord during His public life . . . manifestations which made His teaching so powerful that it changed the world.

Blessed Grignon remarks that God chose to keep His Mother hidden during His public life and during the early life of the Church, even though She was so important in His plan as to be Mediatrix between the world and Himself. But, Blessed Grignon adds, God wishes to make Her known now, in these latter times, so that He can come a second time through Her . . . and this time, more than ever, into our hearts . . .

Few people realize that this second coming of Christ has long been under way. It has been under way since apostolic times, but is merely gaining full momentum today. How long it will take for the full climax to be reached would be difficult to say. Anyone who has found mystical union with Christ through moral union with Mary, has already experienced the "second coming." And when, one Marian dogma after another having been proclaimed, all Catholics will have made "through Mary" their own ascetical formula, then the second coming will have reached its climax.

Today, it is doubtful whether any Catholic truly striving for perfection has not learned that he should seek it through Mary. Books on the subject have been very widely circulated. The Holy Father even attached a plenary indulgence to the reading of a book on the subject, *"True Devotion to the Blessed Virgin,"* by Blessed Grignon de Montfort.

But a *very small percentage* of Catholics are *striving for perfection,* i.e., full union of one's own heart to the Sacred Heart. Most Catholics think it enough to fulfill the Commandments, avoiding mortal sin; to say the morning offering, but not to live it.

It will be the ultimate object of the Scapular Apostolate to make all wearers of the Scapular . . . now about half the total membership of the Church . . . come to a realization of the fact that the Scapular *morally unites them to Mary* and that they should find, through this moral union with the Immaculate Heart of Mary, the bliss of union with the Sacred Heart of Jesus.

"Can anyone fail to see," exclaimed Saintly Pope Pius X, "that there is no surer, no more direct way of uniting all mankind in Christ, than through Mary?"

It must be the object of the Scapular Apostolate to see that the Holy Father's question, at least on the part of Catholics, is answered not only by voice but by action. As an aid, they have Our Lady's own promise of eternal salvation.

Now I have delivered the message, and it is yours.

Author with the Bishop of Fatima.

CHAPTER TWENTY-SIX

Fatima Climax

THE STORY of the Scapular Apostolate told in these pages is just beginning. Things that are written here, and especially in the book *Mary in Her Scapular Promise,* will have far more significance with the passing of each year. The messages of the apparitions of Our Lady at Girkalnis and then in Germany read like a chapter from the latter book. And there is even greater confirmation in the miracle of Fatima.

In 1917 Our Lady appeared to three shepherd children in Fatima, Portugal, and said: "If my requests are heard Russia will be converted and an era of peace will be conceded to humanity."

To prove that Her promise was truly from Heaven Our Lady added that on October 13, 1917, She would perform a public miracle: "That all the world may believe."

Seventy thousand witnesses gathered that day in the Cova da Iria of Fatima. As they fell trembling to their knees the sun danced over their heads in weird motions . . . finally plunging towards the ground.

151

"If my requests are not heard," the Vision said, "there will be another, a more terrible war (World War I was then being fought) beginning in the reign of Pope Pius XI; whole nations will be wiped out; errors from atheist Russia will spread through the whole earth, the good will be persecuted, and the Holy Father will suffer much."

The three requests She made in delivering this ultimatum to the world were:

1) Offering of the sacrifices necessary to fulfillment of daily duty, in reparation and for the conversion of sinners; 2) Recitation of the Rosary with meditation on the mysteries, using fifteen minutes on five consecutive first Saturdays of the month in meditation; 3) Consecration to Her Immaculate Heart ... and She stood in the sky, in the last vision, and held the Brown Scapular down to the World.

In earlier chapters I have said that *Mary in Her Scapular Promise* has never seemed to me to be mine, even though it bears my own name on the title page. I read from it myself, and learn new things. I have sat with study-club groups, and studied it with almost as much a sense of wonder and novelty as any others in the groups. It is a circumstance that my name *is* on the title page ... and, frankly, I have taken advantage of that circumstance to preach the doctrines of Our Blessed Lady with all my heart. This present book is a part of that opportunism ...

Years, and a World War, have come and gone
since the Lay Brother had his "vision" and since
the Scapular Apostolate was founded. The Scapular Magazine has become one of the most accepted
religious periodicals of America, increasing steadily
month after month and year after year at the average rate of more than a thousand new subscribers
with each issue. The half-a-century old church of
Our Lady of the Scapular of Mount Carmel has
emerged from its formerly dismal East-side sur-
roundings and gradually assumes aspects of beauty,
and even the city immediately around it has been
been transformed. Soon people reading these lines,
who may have joined the pilgrims going to that
shrine to pay a visit to the American Madonna of
the Scapular, seeing great new apartment buildings to the south and towering structures housing
United Nations to the north, may wonder that they
should ever have been written. The Shrine . . .
like the world with it . . . has so rapidly changed,
and tens upon tens of thousands of names now rest
there beneath the High Altar for remembrance in
special Saturday votive Masses . . .

Today, there are Scapular headquarters in England
and Spain and France and Australia, and an international headquarters near the Vatican, in Rome.
The Scapular Magazine is now published not only
in New York but also abroad, and has been blessed
with some of the most startling "religious scoops"

of the day. The number of leaflets explaining the
Scapular conditions are numbered in the millions.
The "Morning Offering," which the Brother "received" is now in circulation in almost every nation
of the world and many Catholics are signing pledges
to say it every day. The symbol of the Scapular
Press . . . with the words "The World in the Arms
of Mary" . . . has been duplicated around the entire
globe, it has been copied into the floors of churches,
displayed on letterheads, used again and again in
books and magazines and leaflets . . . in almost unbelievable figures.

And there is a climax:

Upon invitation of the Bishop of Leiria-Fatima, I
visited Sister Lucia Maria das Dores, the visionary
of Fatima, on August 12, 1946. During the conversation I asked Her about the final apparition . . .
the one of Our Lady of Mount Carmel.

The seal mentioned in the book, which came to
being at a time when neither I nor any of our associates knew about Fatima, *has a remarkable resem-
blance to the final apparition of Fatima* . . . where
Our Lady promised (for consecration to Her and
the fulfillment of Her other requests) *the conversion
of Russia and world peace!*

The three requests of Our Lady of Fatima so co-
incide with the three requisites of the Sabbatine
Privilege of the Scapular that *by fulfilling the requests of Fatima one may obtain the privilege* (as-

surance of liberation from Purgatory on the First Saturday after Death). MOREOVER, THE MORNING OFFERING EMBODIES THE PRINCIPAL REQUESTS OF FATIMA.

We learned about Fatima the first time from Archbishop Finbar Ryan, O. P., of Trinidad, B. W. I., who had just read the early edition of *From a Morning Prayer* (to which this and following chapters have been added). After reading it the Archbishop could hardly believe that the apparitions of Fatima . . . most amazing revelation of the Christian era . . . were not even mentioned in it. He was himself the author of one of the first books in the English language on Fatima. So he immediately wrote to us.

"The book *From a Morning Prayer*," he said, "is indeed dynamite . . . to blast apathy towards Our Lady from human hearts! But why do you fail to mention that in Her final appearance at Fatima Our Blessed Lady stood beside the sun, and held the Scapular down to the world?"

Could it be that the origin of the Scapular Apostolate, and the writing of *Mary in Her Scapular Promise* and *From a Morning Prayer*, took place independent of Fatima that the apparitions of Fatima might be a final proof of their message? . . . That, at least, was their effect on myself.

Fatima, of course, is sufficient proof in itself of Our Lady's great desire to see the Scapular . . . the most indulgenced and most miraculous sign of consecration to Her Immaculate Heart . . . spread to the shoulders of every Catholic.

Fatima is the most extraordinary revelation of the Christian era . . . an ultimatum to the world in its "Darkest days (to use the words of Pope Pius XI) since the deluge!" And the final apparition, during which Our Lord stood at Her side and blessed the world while She held down the Scapular, must convince all that we must mark and distinguish ourselves by this sign . . . this seal of being in the arms of Mary.

All that has happened in these previous chapters . . . and especially the fact that the miraculously-given seal of the American Scapular Apostolate should be a picture of the last apparition of Fatima . . . must bear special meaning and special consolation to all who have worked in this Apostolate, because they will know beyond any doubt that they have been following the inspiration of Our Blessed Lady Herself . . . for the speeding of Her Reign and the salvation of the world.

Not long before the time that I am writing this, and a good many years after the earlier chapters of this book were written, the Lay Brother came back . . . after World War II . . . from the foreign mission.

His ship landed in New York City, so I was one of the first to meet him.

He had not changed physically, but his clothing was unbelievably poor. He was smiling. Our handshake spanned the years.

One of the first things we did was to get into an automobile and start for Father John's monastery . . . only about seventy miles away, in the mountains to the west.

When we arrived at the monastery Father John, with the rest of the fathers and clerics, was in choir. We slipped into the back of the chapel and listened to the dignified and rhythmic chant of the Divine Office being recited with the wonderful respect that one would expect in that monastery. It was soon over, and we slipped out to intercept Father John as he walked out of chapel.

Never shall I forget the way his sweet face changed when he saw us . . . how his eyes lighted and his whole being reacted in a little quick raising of the arms which even across distance was an embrace.

Sometime during the next hour, with a twinkle in his eye, the white-haired and venerable Carmelite Novice Master raised his head and said in what seemed to be a slow and very unpremeditated tone:

"Say, Brother, did you ever hear of a book called . . . eh . . . *From a Morning Prayer?*"

I repressed a laugh and was all chuckles inside, but Brother either missing the facetiousness of the tone or else simply considering the matter gravely, turned and said seriously but kindly: "Oh yes," Father, but I would never read that book."

Of course both Father John and I knew well that he would never read it, but if we had hoped that we might find out how much of its contents the good Brother had been told, we were disappointed.

I can very well understand Brother's feelings. I pray that he may ever be spared offense to his humility, and feel sorry for anyone who may ever harm that humility . . . because Our Blessed Lady has so carefully nutured it in him; Her Divine Son must be jealous of it. The book was written under direction and before publication was submitted to a cross-section of critics such as few books have endured, yet I was myself too ashamed ever to open and read it from that day it was published until several years later when it was deemed advisable to add these last chapters.

Still, it was gratifying to note that of more than a hundred reviewers who appraised the book in magazines and newspapers across the nation, only one had any criticism. And when we asked that one to specify his criticism (which was a generality) that we might change the part criticized (which we would have done), he refused to answer. No one will know with what bated breath and misgivings I saw these pages first go to press. Yet now I can see the wisdom of Our Blessed Lady in obtaining all that has been done. Everyone who has participated in the work has been blessed, and sadness has visited many who refused to accept Our Lady's invitation to join with Her final apostolate to bring men, in Her arms of Scapular and Rosary, back to the Sacraments.

God spoke clearly in the garden of Eden when He said to Satan that He placed enmities not only between Satan and Mary, but also between the seed of Satan and Her seed. For indeed, as I heard Father Daniel Lord say, over Her is the world divided, and since the declarations made at Fatima this division will necessarily sharpen.

Lucia with Pope Paul VI at Fatima.

CHAPTER TWENTY-SEVEN

Her Seed and His

TODAY, QUIETLY yet surely, the forces of Mary which have for so many centuries been scattered in many different organizations and under many different titles, are marshalling together against the united forces of Satan.

There are three things which Our Blessed Lady expects today from all Her devotions and all Her organizations, and upon those three things hinges the salvation of the world.

If it be God's Will, another book will supplement this one . . . based on my colloquies with Sister Lucia and reaching through the story of Fatima for its mystery, for its hope. Our Blessed Mother has been very good to me in arranging the contacts necessary for the book . . . including a private interview with the Holy Father, and private sessions not only with Sister Lucia but also with the Bishop of Fatima, with the Cardinal Primate of Portugal, and even with Doctor Salazar, the Portuguese premier.

Therefore I will not speak here at any length about Fatima, and I know that the reader is already well acquainted with the events that took place there in 1917 and of Our Lady's great promise: "If my requests are heard, Russia will be converted, and an era of peace will be conceded to humanity."

But I do want to speak here . . . concerning the forces that work against Our Blessed Lady and the Fatima message.

When Doctor Ralph W. Sockman, the "Monsignor Sheen" of Protestantism, asked me why America had not heard about Fatima before, my answer surprised, and . . . I think . . . repulsed him. Yet I think it is the same answer I would give again: "To my mind it is primarily because not only seventy thousand human witnesses watched the sun miracle at Fatima and heard the dire injunction of the vision, but *the Powers of Hell* were there, too. They have marshalled their force over all the earth to prevent the spread of the Fatima message, and only prayer and sacrifice on the part of the just will bring these diabolical machinations to naught and cause the Fatima message to spread in triumph."

It might have been more circumspect to point out that Fatima took place during World War I, just after the United States entered that first great war, and that the news of the vision was drowned in the noise of Verdun. I might have pointed out, too, that Portugal at the time was ruled by anticlericals, that radio was not developed, that news was comparatively slow, and that the church was at first very reticent about Fatima.

But what would be the genuine and ultimate explanation?

The Powers of Hell are feverishly at work today against Mary and Her seed. Pope Pius XI implied this when he told Father Mateo that our days are *"The darkest since the deluge"*.

Pope Pius XII warned the world, when the year 1946 was turning into the year 1947: "A crisis caused by anti-religious forces is developing in Europe and calls for an extraordinary amount of sacrifice, energy and faith on the part of Christians." *Osservatore Romano,* official Vatican newspaper, said just before Christmas of 1946:

"The struggle *between Christ and anti-Christ* is ever more clearly outlined. Feelings of terror presage *an imminent and appalling battle.* A fearful abyss is seen into which Europe is on the verge of falling."

Our Lady of Fatima pleads for sacrifices for the conversion of sinners, by persons strengthened to that sacrifice through Her Scapular and Rosary. She makes this plea in order that *her power may be unleashed against the power of Satan.*

Only devotion . . . only union with Her Immaculate Heart by the Scapular, and a pouring over of the mysteries of that Heart in the Rosary, can strengthen us to that Sacrifice . . . to avoid sin, fre-

quent the Sacraments. There is real power
working to lead us to sin, to prevent us from fre-
quenting the Sacraments. This power is not only
our fallen nature. It is the power of Hell, now
stronger on the earth than perhaps ever before since
the time of Adam and Eve. (And only conserva-
tism, not personal conviction, persuades me to leave
the word "perhaps" in that statement).

This will be much further elucidated in the book
Flight to Fatima, but I will say here briefly (as I did
at some length in The Scapular Magazine in May,
1946) that I have seen much tangible evidence of
the activity of that power. I saw a project for a
nationwide rededication to the Immaculate Conception on December 8, 1946 (our American centen-
nial of consecration to the Immaculate), which had
cost months of work and thousands of dollars,
crumble overnight. I have had lectures interrupted
(almost always while I was pronouncing the words
"Satan, I shall place enmities between thee and The
Woman . . . ") by a sudden wind crashing open
windows, by a strange disturbance in the audience,
once even by the sound of shrill, cackling laugh-
ter that was heard in the entire hall and drowned
out my voice.

America has been slow to hear the message of
Fatima . . . because there have not been enough of
us in America to pray and to make sacrifices, placing
our trust in Mary's Immaculate Heart, *offering up*

to Her all the sacrifices of our day that She might distribute them to the best interests of the Sacred Heart.

Not long before writing these lines, I was in the Vatican, kneeling in the room next to the Holy Father's study and waiting for His Holiness to enter. I was alone, and stared at the floor thinking.

He came so quickly and silently across the floor that I did not see him until his white cassock was almost touching my hands. And when I looked up, and into his face, my mouth fell open with shock.

I had never seen such suffering.

The Holy Father had just come from his study. He wasn't smiling. And in those deep pools of sadness that were his eyes, and in those heavy lines that dragged at the corners of his mouth, I seemed to see him looking upon those two Catholic-Action priests of Lithuania who were hanging from crosses in a public square; looking upon those signs all over the city of Rome, sporting hammer and sickle and crying in great red letters: "Viva Stalin, Viva Communism!"; looking at bodies in the gutters of Trieste, at the democratic and Christian death of France, where only a few days before I had heard from the lips of a Catholic Action leader in Paris that France was doomed; looking at the piles of corpses of priests and sisters in Albania, Poland, and over an ever rapidly expanding surface of the world

(400 priests had been shot or otherwise killed during the previous ten months in Yugoslavia alone!).

The prophecies of Our Lady of Fatima had all come true . . . and, sadly enough, they were continuing to come true, especially the prophecies: "Several nations will be destroyed, the good will be persecuted, the Holy Father will suffer much, errors from Atheist Russia will spread over the earth . . . "

I could not help but wonder, as does the Holy Father who by radio appealed to mankind for fulfillment of the requests of Fatima as far back as 1942, how long the Powers of Hell will continue to darken the vision of many Catholics who, refusing to be "As little children," look for remedies other than the one remedy of flying beneath the mantle of their Mother . . . where they will be fed by the Sacraments which most of them seem no longer to have the strength to receive.

The three requests of Our Lady of Fatima are intertwined . . . one bearing upon the other. "The most important," Sister Lucia told me, "is sacrifice . . . fulfillment of daily duty . . . and offering these sacrifices necessary to fulfillment of duty for poor sinners."

The secondary requests are Rosary and Scapular . . . and perhaps even more specifically the things which those two devotions demand: Prayerful meditation on the mysteries of the Rosary, and Consecration to the Immaculate Heart.

After hearing both Sister Lucia's and the Bishop's explanation of Fatima, I asked the Bishop: "Your Excellency, why isn't more said about the importance of the Scapular?"

"Here in Portugal," His Excellency replied, "this devotion is universally considered one of the three essential devotions of Fatima, and everyone wears the Scapular."

A lieutenant, professor of History at the Portuguese West Point who was with me in the Bishop's chambers, vigorously nodded his head, tapped his uniformed chest significantly and echoed: "Everybody in Portugal wears the Brown Scapular."

Unfortunately this is far from true in the United States.

IF WE APOSTLES WORK EARNESTLY ENOUGH, thereby doing "more than our share," Russia will be converted and there will be peace *before* America has to walk down the same road as Poland and Yugoslavia, Roumania and Russia, Lithuania and parts of Germany. This is what Sister Lucia said:

"I think that the next thing that will happen will be that the Holy Father, and all the Bishops, will make a special consecration of Russia to the Immaculate Heart of Mary."

"And then, Sister," I asked, "will Russia be converted, and will there be peace?"

"Yes," she answered, "that is what Our Blessed

Lady promised."

"And *when,* Sister," I begged, "when will this happen?"

"WHEN A SUFFICIENT NUMBER ARE OF-FERING THEIR SACRIFICES AND FULFIL-LING OUR LADY'S REQUESTS," she answered.

It may be that you, reading these lines, may be or *may obtain* the VERY LAST OF THAT SUFFI-CIENT NUMBER, and we will see a wonder over Russia greater than the wonder over Fatima in 1917 that caused 70,000 people to fall in the mud and cry "My God, have mercy on us!" and there will be peace.

And, oh! . . . in the name of Heaven . . . *don't* lay this book aside without having made up your mind to do *something*—something more than you have already done.

Take a look at the world and ask yourself: *"How much time do we have?"*

The Promise of Our Lady of Fatima is our only chance. "Only the Blessed Virgin," She said, "can save the world."

What YOU, reading these lines, do today . . . may make Her promise come true TOMORROW.

And your own reward will be boundless . . .

The most powerful Fatima force in the world today, with millions of members from almost every nation outside the Iron Curtain, is the Blue Army of Our Lady of Fatima. Above, before a poster which repeats words of Pope Pius XII to Fatima apostles, laymen speak at Blue Army Congress in July, 1953. At lower left, Father Colgan...founder of the Blue Army, places box of microfilm with almost half a million names in ground beneath tree in the Cova da Iria at Fatima. New names are added constantly. At lower right is actual photo of the Pilgrim Virgin in Moscow. Through window behind statue, Kremlin towers are visible. Much of story behind it is still unknown, but Blue Army was largely responsible.

CHAPTER TWENTY-EIGHT

TWENTY-FIVE YEARS LATER

THE PREVIOUS CHAPTERS, written before 1947, cover happenings of less than a decade. So the reader can imagine how much more has happened in the ensuing quarter of a century.

However a few events most relevant to our story may quickly be told.

The Provincial who refused to accept me for solemn vows (for a reason which had nothing to do with me personally) would probably have been the General of the Order. He was a brilliant man, fluent in thirteen languages, a likeable foreshadowing of the post Vatican II priests of the right. But he died in a foreign mission and his last words, just before he died, were "John Haffert." I don't know whether he was thinking of Father John or me. I think it must have been both.

That may not seem very mysterious to the reader, but it is one of the significant "untold" parts of the story.

We could have told it twenty-five years ago. And

someone whom I had to see almost every day said to me, and over and over: "There must be something wrong with you. The Carmelites threw you out." But not even to that person was an explanation given. And now that so many years have passed, and death has intervened, we still leave it half told.

If there is one great personal lesson of this story, it is the lesson of confidence in God, of obedience to His Will as manifested through *whatever* legitimate church authority.

The Brother believed this so completely that I don't think it was ever even difficult for him. And though I suffered the dislocation or humiliation of the moment, I know it was never too difficult for me. God is our Father, and would He give us something not good for us?

But leaving the monastery in 1937 (I think the Brother's vision was in 1933) was not as difficult as what happened in 1948.

I had brought the Pilgrim Virgin to America only a few months before without asking permission of Cardinal Spellman. It had never even occurred to me to ask him because it was the purpose of the Pilgrim Virgin to go to ANY diocese to which it was invited. But it certainly would have been prudent for me to have asked the Cardinal first.

When I sensed opposition to the Pilgrim Virgin in New York, I offered it to Archbishop Vachon, in Canada, who received it with tremendous display.

The motorcade from the airport was miles long and thousands gathered at the Cathedral in Ottawa, where the Archbishop crowned Our Lady and consecrated his diocese and Canada to her as Queen of the World.

Bishop O'Hara of Buffalo (later Cardinal of Philadelphia) then asked for the statue and it entered the United States on Dec. 8th, 1947, with such acclaim that the police of the city said it resulted in the greatest traffic jams in the city's records. Bishop O'Hara was himself so impressed that he offered to head the pilgrimage for the entire United States and to offer the visit to any of the Bishops who desired it when they all met in Washington, D. C., for the annual Bishop's meeting.

He spoke of the Pilgrim Virgin and its meaning. He offered the statue to any Bishop who would wish to "sign up" for it. When he finished "One of the Cardinals opposed the idea." As a result, NOT ONE BISHOP asked for the statue . . . but in the cloakroom, after the meeting, Bishop Waters of Raleigh, N. C., said: "John, you can send it to me."

After Raleigh it went to a neighboring diocese, and then another, and another . . . and the wave of devotion swept through all America until almost EVERY BISHOP finally had received the statue and laid his crosier and mitre at Our Lady's feet.

I suppose this was a sort of humiliation to Cardinal Spellman who was a real "stickler" for having anything cleared through him. They said that his office on Madison Avenue was the U. S. Vatican. In any event, our apostolate in New York (with a magazine reaching perhaps half a million readers) was the big force behind the Pilgrim Virgin, and suddenly the Carmelite Provincial got a letter from Madison Avenue suggesting that he should replace the layman running that apostolate.

It was a Friday afternoon in midsummer.

It was as though I were being offered a blindfold and told to walk the plank.

It never even occurred to me to go to the Cardinal. The note was definite and final.

This rupture carried a far greater sense of heartbreak than when I left the Carmelite Order just as I was about to take solemn vows.

Ten years had passed . . . and in that decade I had found the way of fulfilling my vocation. Over a million dollars had been given by little and ordinary persons all over America, and the magazine (started in 1940) had a circulation now of over 150,000 copies each issue. The Pilgrim Virgin campaign and "March of Pledges" were in full swing.

This "March" netted almost *one and a half million* signed promises to wear the Scapular and say the Rosary daily in addition to making the Morning Offering and living it through the day!

But obviously pride had entered in . . . and I was seeing myself in the work, like a speaker who, although giving the message, is also taking pleasure in the sound of his own voice. Pretty soon such a speaker is only a voice; the message doesn't come through.

The heartbreak was compounded by an awareness that I was not holy enough, that God had taken me out of the great work given so gloriously in the Brother's vision, and in addition I had not saved any money to feed my wife and a little baby (just adopted at this identical moment in time). I would have to take up a whole new career although my heart and soul and mind were all absorbed in a work which totally occupied me up to one moment on a Friday afternoon, but was over Friday night. When I came on Monday to pick up some papers from my desk, another man was there . . . and I was told that it was better that I should take no papers. Whatever was really personal would be sent.

Even my books . . . which had sold well . . . and were not "mine," because I had not wanted to have a personal interest in them. Any money I received from lectures and books I had turned into the apostolate. I did not feel it belonged to me. My total salary when I started was $35 a week, and while I do not remember now just what it was when I left, it was at least not more than I needed to live. I worked for God and I trusted in Him.

I can't say that this trust wavered during this trial. But I did come close to a nervous breakdown, partly because of the trial and partly because I had been overworking just prior to it.

I do not think my wife EVER recovered from this experience.

I wrote in despair to the Brother and told him that my work was over although I had not accomplished all that I had envisioned.

He wrote back: "This is only a time of trial. After a wait, your greatest work lies ahead."

For the first time in my life I did not believe him.

From New York the author moved to this farm in New Jersey where the Pilgrim Virgin was kept until it went to Russia in 1950. Building was later converted into what is now Ave Maria Institute, National U.S.A. Centre of the Blue Army of Our Lady.

CHAPTER TWENTY-NINE

ANOTHER START, ANOTHER TRIAL

SOMEWHAT "secretly" I had brought not one Pilgrim Virgin to America, but two. The second was somehow to be gotten into Russia.

I prepared an oratory in a room over the garage on a poor farm in New Jersey to which I had moved my family as soon as possible after leaving New York. Father John came all the way from Chicago to install the statue but he was seized with such a terrible attack of neuralgia that he had to return to Chicago.

I then remembered having lectured in Saint Mary's Parish, in Plainfield, N. J., and how impressed I was with the pastor there who had asked everyone in his parish (who joined the March of Pledges) to "Wear something blue" so that they would "stand up and be counted as on Our Lady's side in the struggle with the powers of evil." He had said from the pulpit: "We will be the Blue Army of Our Lady against the Red Armies of atheism."

Because of my mental state, I did not want anyone whom I did not completely trust to know about the statue for Russia. That's why I had asked Father John to come all the way from Chicago. Now it occurred to me that Father Colgan of Plainfield was one I could trust. And I invited him.

Two weeks later I happened to meet Father Daniel Lord who had cited Father Colgan as one of the most outstanding Sodalist-priests in America. And I asked him:

"Father, what would you think if I joined up with Father Colgan to promote the message of Fatima?"

And Father Lord's answer was prophetic:

"There will be an explosion for Our Lady."

It was the Carmelite Fathers who supplied the means. After considerable study, they decided to pay me $10,000 for work I had done in New York, for book royalties, etc., and gave me back the rights to all the books I had written . . . and even a supply of copies they had on hand. This was the generous work of Fr. Sylvester Maher (mentioned in the first acknowledgments to this book) and to the same Provincial who had the unhappy task of dropping me from the Scapular Apostolate.

Father Colgan and I published the first issue of SOUL Magazine in January of 1950, using less than eight hundred names as a foundation . . . mostly names of "followers" who had somehow found me and written. Just before, I got a call from the Assumptionist Fathers saying that Stalin, after refusing a Catholic priest the visa he had promised to Roosevelt for services to Embassy Personnel, had granted the visa and they would take the statue to Russia.

It seemed more than symbolic (like the Pilgrim Virgin itself) that the statue which the old Bishop had blessed for Russia, while two other statues traveled around the world, should go to Moscow as the "March of Pledges" turned into a "Blue Army of Our Lady of Fatima." Just one year later, in an address to the world but beamed especially to more than a million persons gathered at Fatima, Pope Pius XII was to say:

"In 1946 I crowned her here at Fatima as QUEEN OF THE WORLD, and through the Pilgrim Virgin she went forth AS THOUGH TO CLAIM HER DOMINION. And the favors she performs along the way (and the Holy Father mentioned the United States) are such THAT WE CAN HARDLY BELIEVE WHAT WE ARE SEEING WITH OUR EYES."

Bishop Sheen was at Fatima that day and he said to the Press: "The white square of Fatima has already overcome the Red Square of Moscow . . . only the news hasn't leaked out yet."

I was still concerned about the Scapular Apostolate in New York. I had wanted very much to have two or three lay brothers to train for the work, but my departure was so abrupt that of course there was not time to "pass on" the little I had learned in the ten years since I had left the seminary.

But it would seem that the Scapular Apostolate was only a first phase of the fulfillment of the Brother's vision. It faded. The policy of the Scapular magazine was changed. Today it no longer exists.

But the Blue Army has spread and is now recognized as the OFFICIAL Fatima apostolate of the world. In a meeting of the International Council in 1970, in its 120 room International Centre at Fatima, the leaders evaluated their membership at more than twenty million, in seventy countries. There is another international office in Switzerland and there are centres in most major nations of the world.

By 1960 the Blue Army had already become one of the most powerful Marian apostolates in America. It had a television program on some one hundred stations, a weekly program in New York, and was going "full blast" to convince enough persons of the reality of the promise made at Fatima:

If enough persons make this pledge and keep it, *"Russia will be converted and an era of peace will be conceded to mankind."*

Then, again, the ceiling fell in.

My wife had been more deeply affected by the abrupt change in our lives in 1948 than anyone realized. She had a five month old baby, was suddenly whisked to an old farm house on a dirt road with no neighbors, and did not know what provision would be made for tomorrow . . . or whether I might get involved in some other apostolic work, and again some superior might say "I prefer that you drop this" and we would be plunged again into nothingness.

So a short time after the Blue Army started, while I was on a trip she rented out the house on the farm and moved into an apartment in New York. And for the next six years I worked on the farm. (I tried to open a "convenience office" in New York, but Cardinal Spellman told me to close it.) I had to commute sixty miles each way to see my family. And as the years passed it became increasingly difficult. Meanwhile the baby became a willowy child . . . and the New York apartment happened to be on 84th Street, which in 1960 had the highest crime rate of any street in the city of New York; and our daughter was walking those blocks to and from school, alone.

I put my foot down . . . without sufficient understanding or gentleness. I had no idea of my wife's own real feelings and mental state. That apartment was now "home" to her and she could not think of leaving New York again. She went to a lawyer. He said she could keep the apartment only if she got a separation. And he prepared papers for her. And the newspapers got hold of it. One, with a circulation of over five million, gave it a major banner headline!

And that very day the major networks were to

view a just completed television series (CRISIS)
which had cost us half a million dollars, featuring
President Kennedy in person in no less than three of
the half-hour programs.

No one showed up for the showing . . . except one
out-of-town reporter who hadn't seen the news.

(Oddly enough, it was Cardinal Spellman who
came to the rescue . . . because he got inside reports
on the whole matter and with the tremendous influence he had in the city of New York, the entire matter was settled. Shortly before he died he wrote me
a letter, saying the he was going to recommend my
book on the Eucharist to all his priests.)

Very often we think it is the Communists who are
behind the worst conflicts we encounter in our apostolate. And in this instance, especially with the deliberate "leak" to the press which appalled my wife
as much as it did me, there may have been such inter-
ference.

But this was the third time in my life that the pain
was so great that I prayed to die . . . not just because
of the pain, but because in the pain I felt close to Our
Lord and it would have been a happy time to die.

This time I did not write to Brother and lament
that all was over. I resigned from the Blue Army,
in the face of the scandal.

To my surprise, the Bishop and the Trustees refused my resignation.

CHAPTER THIRTY

Brother Was Praying

Of course the television show fell through. By the time the noise died down, the material of the program was stale.

And I had a very difficult domestic adjustment. My wife had accepted the decision of the court to give up the New York apartment, but that did not make it any easier for her to again adjust her life. When she first came back to the farm she could not even bring herself to enter the house.

In this extremity I felt that a radical change was needed. Since Vatican Council II was just opening I decided to go to Rome.

We rented an apartment there, and for the following six years Rome was my second home. And meanwhile I tried to make a house on the farm which my wife and daughter would enjoy using.

It was a Providential move.

Not only did I finally succeed in writing the WORLD'S GREATEST SECRET, but I saw a great deal of the Bishops of the world, I came close to the Bishop of Fatima, I came close to the heart of the Church.

And our family began to heal and to knit together again. Somehow, even though we never gave any explanation to anyone (what is being printed here is a "FIRST") the scandal blew over. There is no doubt that it set back the Blue Army apostolate . . . but only like a hesitation step. Msgr. Colgan made a public statement simply affirming his support and indicating that the allegations in the press were not true. For many this was enough. For those who opposed the apostolate of Fatima . . . scant comfort was gained because the movement began to gain momentum in other parts of the world.

What the Brother had received (a message saved for our time) turned out to be the message of Fatima IN ITS APPLICATION. And little by little sensible men everywhere have come to realize that unless the message is applied, the promise of peace cannot be obtained.

Of all the little things that have happened in these past twenty-five years I never expect to write the story. What I find most interesting (like losing a schooner in a storm off of Charleston in May of 1968 or walking through the raindrops at Lourdes) might seem trivial or even ridiculous to many. I am sure I could never recapture the simplicity with which I first wrote this book. Now I am self-conscious about all that has happened and much more aware that I am a weak and sinful man, and I should not be writing such a story in the first place if it were not for Father John suffering months on end with the most painful form of neuralgia; for Brother being humiliated and tried beyond what I would have considered possible; for my Sister suffering a trial in Carmel which . . . despite the comfort and support of her community . . . was perhaps the most awful cross she could have had; and for many other "saints" whom I met along the way.

Perhaps I find this book embarrassing (after writing it 25 years ago in somewhat childish enthusiasm) because details of such a personal experience may give the impression I am "special."

I remember that after a four-hour interview with Lucia (who saw Our Lady of Fatima) I took leave of her without any particular sense of "awe" because I somehow knew that she did not feel special even though she had been the object of an historic supernatural intervention. Then suddenly the person with me reached out to touch a rosary to her hand. She recoiled as though stung by nettles. Her eyes, though mild as a dove's, seemed to blaze for a moment in a displeasure that cried: "Why would you want to honor one who is no more than you?"

And the same sort of malaise strikes me at the turn of almost every page of this book . . . although its truths and half-truths are an effort to tell a story which had to be told. I wrote it in two weeks, like a child blurting out a secret that couldn't be kept. I see the crisis in the world today as primarily a crisis of faith.

Some great minds, in postconciliar questioning of what had once been taken purely on faith, seem to be temporarily losing contact with God as they seek new contacts and new forms of expression. From this lack of contact we have a moral crisis. And at Fatima children were chosen to establish contact for us all . . . and even to turn back the Russian based powers of militant atheism.

I once made a retreat under the famous Father Gannon (President of Fordham University) considered in my time as one of the greatest preachers in the Church. I asked him what ONE piece of advice he would give to an intellectual who wanted to really find Christ.

He said he had none. But he recalled the words of Our Lord: "Unless you become as little children . . ."

We in the West are engaged, in many of our universities, in titanic mental battles over the existence of God (reflected also in a moral crisis). But there are hundreds of thousands who have been RAISED AS ATHEISTS behind an Iron Curtain who will come forth and give a new language of faith to the next generation. There will be whole new world. And it will not come through argument, through criticism of the Church, through seeking one's "own thing."

It will be the triumph announced to children: of the Immaculate Heart of Mary.

"In the end," she said, "My Immaculate Heart will triumph, Russia will be converted and there will be peace."

There is nothing wrong with stretching the muscles of the mind against the mystery of Absolute Being. But there is wrong in denial of either the Absolute Being or contingent being simply because WE don't understand how both can be.

St. Therese of Lisieux had a good mind. Pius XI called her the "Messenger of the Twentieth Century." And it is her kind of message we all need and that Fatima wants us to hear.

I was on a cruise with a nonbeliever. There were just the two of us in a schooner at sea. It was inevitable that we should get to know each other's deeper thoughts. And I found that he did not believe because he never knew what God was, or Who Christ is. And I sometimes wonder whether more harm has not been done by the *wrong* kind of spiritual books and teaching than by religion's enemies.

Could there be any greater deterrent to union with Our Lord than a misconception of Him as a "cross-giver"? Can anyone fail to see that sin and suffering and death are the wages of sin . . . and that the crosses that sin impose on us are LIGHTED by Christ, who came to SHARE them with us, to repair for the sins, to give hope and meaning to it all?

Children can understand this!

I have never found that being able to discuss Chardin, even in a few different languages, ever helped anyone half a degree to closer contact with God. The discussions may be necessary, and they may lead somewhere, and people of faith should try to understand those who don't have it.

But the message of Fatima (given to and understood by three children!) is like a new Sinai. It was confirmed at a predicted time and place by a public miracle more dramatic and compelling than any atomic explosion. It makes a fresh statement of the essential Old and New Testament commandments. And whether our minds be like "blanks" emerging through an Iron Curtain, or littered by a Western maze of arguments and doubts and misconceptions, we will solve crises of the atomic age only by accepting those commandments.

Lay apostles may be of great help in calling the attention of the world to this new Sinai . . . and in helping to destroy today's golden calf of materialism.

Perhaps the ordination of deacons is going to help

in the future. Lay apostles have to be educated and qualified. They need training in ascetical theology. An occasional lecture or mission cannot substitute for the science of the saints. Older persons can acquire it through years of daily Mass and Communion, but those who assume leadership when they are young have to know at least the basics of dogmatic and ascetical theology. I'd love to see a training school of this kind . . . a sort of "one year novitiate" for the lay apostolate.

Would it be too extreme to say that one of the best opportunities today to follow the advice of Our Lord might be found in the lay apostolate?

Our Lord said to seek God's Will . . . to seek "His Kingdom" . . . and that everything else would be taken care of (Matt. VI, 33). And would it not seem that the major point here is not so much the question of property but of security? If I have all the things I need for my use, it makes little difference whether I own them myself or in common if I cannot be suddenly "dumped out" on my own. And today Church Law protects religious. Some priests are organizing unions, in addition to having the right to acquire personal wealth.

But a layman who serves in an apostolate . . . without any guarantee of security and with too small a salary to provide adequately for it himself . . . may expect to hear at any time (even after years of service): "We don't need you now," or "We have

a new superior and he'd rather have his own help"
or "Thanks for all you've done but we now have a
priest or a brother or a sister who can take this
over now."

A layman must enter the apostolate WITH THIS
KIND OF EXPECTATION rather than the expectation of a secure future!

I cannot say that this was not a trial for me, but
I think I can sincerely say that I never REALLY
worried. I believed that if I sincerely tried to do
what I understood God wanted of me, that He was
my Father . . . . and that was that.

I think it is a shame . . . a *real* shame . . . that we
seem to have lost in this security-seeking world of
ours this glorious sense of serving God with an aban-
doned trust. How many capable and educated men
are willing to dedicate themselves to religious work?
Can we believe it is because God has failed to CALL
them? or is there just not enough faith to enable His
Voice to be heard?

It is all in taking the FIRST step. After that it
is a day to day matter of refreshment and strength
in Holy Communion, made ever more intimately and
fruitfully through union with the Immaculate Heart
of Mary obtained by such simple means as living up
to all that is implied in her devotions of the Rosary
and the Scapular. And then we just have to watch
out that we don't attribute to ourselves what must be
attributed to God . . .

When a work like the Legion or the Blue Army sweeps over the world, it is GOD's work. And no matter how involved, who could think of it in ANY WAY as a personal achievement? And if he should (and perhaps I have) . . . he can expect to have a Cardinal to say "It would be better that this man be dropped," or he can expect to be cut down in his tracks when he least expects it.

One day, sometime between 1948 and 1950, I asked the Brother:

"You know that I am your voice. God is protecting you and keeping you hidden while I have to be out in front doing the work. And do you pray for me?"

He said he did.

"But I know you pray for MANY things, Brother," I insisted, "but do you pray for ME?"

And he replied: "Every day, since that 'experience,' *I mention you by name at the elevation in the Mass.*"

And today, people who spend a length of time at Fatima, may often wonder about the Carmelite priest seen so often (at most daily Masses) in the Basilica of Fatima, or praying at the Chapel of the Apparitions . . . and it is Father Gabriel Pausback . . . the same Assistant General who was cofounder of the Scapular Apostolate and who spends his life at Fatima now in writing and prayer . . . and every once in awhile we embrace, and he will ask "How is Anne?", and it seems as though the years haven't happened.

And my sister suffered in Carmel, and offered it for success. And God has spared Father John even until now . . . not to glory in what has been achieved, but to continue to pray and suffer for its success. My mother had a beautiful death in 1970 and my father carries on.

And what an incredible success the apostolate continues to be! Above all there is the growth of the "hours of holiness" in the Blue Army, and the all night vigils. People by the tens of thousands have literally lived the Morning Offering through the Blue Army pledge. The "wordless prayer" has become a way of life for millions.

One evidence of the success was the world-wide coronation of Our Lady in 1971 when on the same day, for seventy countries around the world, Bishops joined in crowning Our Lady. The Holy Father participated in a message by radio and television. It was perhaps the greatest manifestation in honor of the Blessed Virgin on a single day in history.

I mention this, out of all the wonderful things that have happened, because this world-wide coronation was not just an affirmation of the Queenship of Mary through the Blue Army, but it was a world-wide act of consecration to Her Immaculate Heart . . . because if the world recognizes her as Queen, it recognizes her right to our honor and service.

And do you know where I was on that May 13th? I was in Moscow . . . for the crowning of that Pilgrim Virgin statue which went there in 1950, when the work of the Blue Army began. One of the crowns seen on the front cover of this book was solemnly placed on the statue by a Legate of the Bishop of Fatima. And persons from all six continents of the world were present either on the day we brought the crown or on the day of the crowning (May 12th-13th). The Holy Father was speaking at that moment by radio and television about the honor to the QUEEN OF THE WORLD and not only were official coronations being held by Bishops for seventy different countries, but hundreds of diocesan and parochial coronations were being held at the same moment.

Who would have thought it possible?

Coronation of the Pilgrim Virgin in Moscow, May 13th, 1971. Representatives assisted from five continents.

CHAPTER THIRTY-ONE

"All Other Things"

FROM THE BEGINNING I felt that a work as important as that conveyed by Brother had to have more sacrifice and prayers behind it than even he, or my sister and uncle, or all my friends could muster. I had to find saints. And I made a conscious effort to do so. I cultivated the acquaintance of devout people. When I wrote THE WORLD'S GREATEST SECRET I had over two hundred persons offering their daily Mass and Communion for the book. I went to Paray le Monial for prayers, and I asked Father Pio several times. And through the years I longed to have a community of Prayer and adoration at the American Headquarters of the Blue Army (Ave Maria Institute) to back up the apostolate.

This longing was gloriously fulfilled on Dec. 8th, 1970, when Bishop Ahr blessed a cornerstone for a HOUSE OF PRAYER, with a chapel exactly reproducing the Holy House of Nazareth. And the Felician Sisters, who had been founded for honor to the Eucharist through the Immaculate Heart of Mary, came to carry out the program of this "House of Prayer."

Just the story of this community coming . . . and how the Foundress had come eighteen years before and placed in the ground a statue of Saint Joseph . . . would fill a book like this one.

God's Providence? What person of faith could fail to put ALL trust in so loving, so Provident a Father? And how I regret all those books about God chastising those He loves, and how we must carry the cross to be with Jesus . . . WITHOUT MENTIONING THE JOYS, THE TRIUMPHS, THE CONSTANT TRANQUILITY OF SPIRIT that attends His service!

Once I was riding in a train in Portugal with one of the world's wealthiest men. He had gone with me to Coimbra in the hopes of seeing Lucia. But the Carmel said that I could see her, but no one else.

As we rode towards Lisbon, I suddenly realized that I was more fortunate than my companion who could command millions of dollars!

And I remembered the tears my father shed those not so many years ago when I told him I did not want to go into his business because I had something special to do . . . A Carmelite Brother had had a real vision, and I was supposed to make his message known to the world . . . and God would provide.

Crosses? Sure. You've read three times in this book that I prayed to die. But I'm not at all sure that those were not THE HAPPIEST MOMENTS OF ALL, deep, deep down.

Will there be more crosses?

I hope so . . . if by crosses you mean those tests which give us a chance to tell Our Lord REALLY that be believe, we adore, we trust, we love Him!

An "unseen" but certainly crucial test, from beginning to end, is the use of money.

I don't know how well the thought came through in the earlier part of this book, but from the beginning I wanted somehow to support myself while fulfilling the mission of Brother's message.

My original feelings in this regard never changed. I reckoned the minimum amount I needed. Without allowing any provision for the future other than life insurance (for my wife and daughter) I limited my salary in the apostolate to that amount. To this day it never exceeded $100 a week.

In the sixties and into the seventies this was inadequate. But by then, through outside work and investments (especially in property) I was so well-to-do that I was myself the largest single contributor to my own apostolate.

Some time in the sixties, the Institute inaugurated a pension plan for its employees. I felt that social justice demanded this. But I deliberatedly excluded myself from the program because it was against my principles. The agent in charge of the project tried to convince me, and then he went to Msgr. Colgan and the Trustees and had me included "over my head" as it were, and even without my knowledge.

I have always felt that in an apostolate it is of PARAMOUNT IMPORTANCE to preserve purity of motive. I always took literally the words of Our Lord:

"Seek first the kingdom of Heaven, and *all these things shall be added unto you.*"

I know that some scriptural experts say that the phrase is not to be taken literally, but I cannot agree. Not from my own instincts, and certainly not from my own experience. Is not our purity of motive tested primarily in the fact that we DO seek God's Will first, last, and always . . . *trusting in Him* for all the rest? And for a person in an apostolate, is not this purity of motive somewhat like bodily purity, requiring the same exercise of prayer and prudence? One may fail from this moment to that, but there can be no failure in the premeditated acts, such as setting a salary or deciding what belongs to the apostolate and what does not.

I learned an early discipline which stood me in good stead.

Between 1948 and 1952, when I was very poor and the Blue Army needed every penny I could get, there was always a temptation to open the envelope received after a lecture to see how much it contained. So I made it a practice to wait until the next day . . . and then, with prayers said and a new program ahead, I found it didn't matter, in the least.

Once I gave a talk in Dayton, Ohio, and the sponsors were the wealthy Sherman family. They gave me a little package after the lecture and as was my custom I didn't open it.

The next day, when I did, I found a beautiful wallet with my name engraved on a sliver plate, with $500 inside. Fortunately I had opened it before I left Dayton and was able to thank them for great thoughtfulness. Miss Sherman, with obvious relief, said: "Oh, we are so glad you like it. When you did not mention it we were afraid perhaps we had given too little!"

One reason this is a delicate subject is because it is quite personal. And another is because . . . as in the case of bodily purity . . . it is (as I say repeatedly in my book SEX AND THE MYSTERIES) not so much an area of black and white decisions, but of a grey fog in which our sincerity is constantly tested. And the big tests in this regard certainly come especially in the time of youth. Some young people preoccupied with thoughts of future benefits and security may hear Christ saying to them:

"But if you want to be perfect, sell all . . . and follow Me . . ."

What a hard saying in today's world! And those who take Our Lord literally are certain to have their sincerity put to an early test.

St. Anthony Mary Claret won great sainthood through overcoming ONE major temptation against purity in his teens. For Blessed Anne Marie Taigi,

I think the great test came when she was only ten, and she made an heroic act to protect the Pope on his journey to meet Emperor Joseph.

God is our Father, and would we expect Him to trust us with His Kingdom . . . or to spoil us . . . without first testing our motives?

Today I feel embarrassed by the amount of wealth I have accumulated, even though it has been independent of the apostolate and has taken only "extra" time. But I consider this abundance as one of the greatest evidences of God's ineffable Gentleness and Kindness, constantly fulfilling Our Lord's Promise about "All those things."

Can the reader imagine how I would feel . . . day after day . . . if I were compensated like a secular executive by an apostolate to which even one widow's mite was contributed?

Can you imagine what it must mean to me, having to write appeals for such things as the redemption of the Icon of Kazan (which we are giving back to Russia) or a seminar for priests at Fatima or new centres in India . . . knowing that I can myself be a contributor?

Can this be described as anything but the LAVISH love of a Heavenly Father?

I know now that I wasn't wrong when I felt, like Saint Paul in Corinth, that I should work "on the side" to earn instead of expecting gifts or miracles. The miracles are always there if needed. But no

Father wants to support a child who isn't sincere or willing to work.   There would often be the question: "Was this for me personally, or was it merely because I am a servant of God?"

If the latter, it belongs to the Master, not to me. And I could think of nothing more harmful to my intimacy with God than to abuse His calling to be His servant. Could a later gift, even a thousand times greater, make amends for such a fault?

To conclude this subject, there remains one question: "If it is better to have the best professionals in apostolic work instead of less competent 'volunteers,' then why look for 'apostles'? why not just get professionals to do the job?"

The answer is that the *leadership* has to be dedicated.

Top professionals in publicity and public relations (which is basically what an apostolate is) will not have the spirit and background of the apostolate. They can handle a personality, a corporate image, a product. But when it comes to God's intervention in the world . . . they must have the inspiration and direction of someone totally dedicated. Without purity of motive and true holiness at the head, an apostolate will most certainly fail.

An apostolate is not a business. It is an unseen battle being waged. The forces of this battle are titanic. The conversion of Russia and the peace of the entire world are at stake. A Woman is crushing a serpent . . . and that serpent is adored by more than half the world.

With my own ears I heard the saintly Capuchin, Father Pio (who for fifty years bore in his body the bleeding wounds of Our Lord) say:

"Russia will be converted when there is a Blue Army member for every Communist."

If Father Pio was right, the devil knows it. He knows that if enough people take up the simple devotions of the Rosary and the Scapular and live the morning offering, they will be united to the Immaculate Heart of Mary . . . and draw the Holy Spirit into the world as into a new cenacle. Some of the fullness of Grace in the Heart of Mary will be flooded into the world, completely reversing the atmosphere of godlessness.

The reader can imagine how I must feel . . . having written this book BEFORE I EVER HEARD OF FATIMA . . . to see in it now the basis of what has become the official Fatima apostolate of the world.

In a sense this book is the story of the book written before it: MARY IN HER SCAPULAR PROMISE (now published under the title SIGN OF HER HEART).

The last edition of this book, with liberal quotations from Lucia (whom Our Lady left on earth to explain her message), was translated into Portuguese in Lucia's own Carmel, in Coimbra (Portugal). The preface was written by the late Bishop of Coimbra who was the same prelate to raise the question, during Vatican II, that the Rosary be specified in Paragraph 67 of *Lumen Gentium*. In that preface His Excellency wrote:

"But the Scapular of Carmel is a reality among those 'practices and exercises of piety which, in honor of Mary, the Magisterium of the Church has recommended through the centuries' (*Lumen Gentium*, 67) and which the Council also recommends today."

Lucia had said that the Rosary and Scapular were inseparable devotions. And Pope Paul VI, in his exhortation to the XI International Marian Congress, a few months after *Lumen Gentium* was promulgated, singled out these same two devotions above all others . . . explaining that they should be spread through the Church today and practiced in depth.

The great importance of this will be seen in the epilogue which follows.

For those who know all this, is there not a great responsibility to become involved? And if this book says anything . . . it says that those who *do* become involved will find a satisfaction and joy they could not have imagined.

And Our Lady's Fatima Promise will come true.

Apostolate of Holiness

In 1531 Our Lady appeared in the principal city of America clothed in white, blue and brown and praying in the sun. In the same colors she appeared in the sun at Fatima: "So that everyone may believe".

The importance of Fatima staggers the imagination. It confirms the "prophecies" and recent teaching of saints like Peter Julian Eymard, Grignion de Montfort, John Bosco, and so many others. It is like a climax to all the Marian apparitions since four hundred years ago... when Our Lady gave to the world a portrait of herself praying in the sun.

Six experts, appointed by the Bishop of Fatima in 1968, are now studying which elements of the message of Fatima are most important. They have a difficult task because the message is complex. As Cardinal Tedeschini said when he came to Fatima as legate of Pius XII in 1951: "Fatima is an affirmation of the gospel". And it is deeply linked with both the past and the future.

Some experts feel that Fatima can be understood only in relation to all the Marian apparitions which have preceded it. They feel that each apparition, after the "portrait apparition" in Mexico, conveys part of the total message given to the world at Fatima. Others feel that there are still important elements Lucia may clarify before she dies, or that may be made public after her death.

All agree, however, that

Above, Lucia (with whose help the Blue Army pledge was written) with Pope Paul VI at Fatima, May 13, 1967.

Fatima is of staggering importance. It is a supernatural intervention at a critical moment of history.

Claudel called it "An explosion of the supernatural".

Many relate this intervention to the threat of worldwide atomic war. They substantiate this by the prophecy of Our Lady that "entire nations will be annihilated" and by the miracle of the sun, recalling that when the President of the United States first announced the bombs dropped on Nagasaki and Hiroshima, he said that man had learned "to use the power of the sun". And it is capable of destroying "entire nations".

Many Elements

Obviously, with a message of such great importance, the world could not wait to know at least the essentials required by God at this hour to turn back the tide of Communism and to bring into the world an atmosphere of God's Grace and of international peace. In general, they were stated clearly at the very time of the apparitions:

"Men must cease offending God, Who is already so much offended."

But we were also exhorted to reparation, penance, the Rosary, sacrifices for sinners, specific prayers taught by angels, consecration to the Immaculate Heart of Mary, devotion to the Immaculate Heart of Mary, and a devotion which had begun shortly before in the Church: The five first Saturdays consisting of rosary, meditation on rosary mysteries for fifteen minutes, confession and communion, all in reparation to the Immaculate Heart of Mary on five consecutive first Saturdays. Finally there was the demand for the consecration of Russia to the Immaculate Heart of Mary.

What Is Basic

The ability to sift out exactly what the INDIVIDUAL Catholic had to do was further complicated by the fact that some parts of this message were made public in 1917, but other parts were withheld until many years later. Indeed, the last major apparition to Lucia... in which the sign for the conversion of Russia was given... took place in June, 1929. It was made known to Pope Pius XII only in 1940! It first became known to the world when it was published by the Bishop of Fatima in 1967, Jubilee year of Fatima, in a booklet containing the official transcript of Lucia's own words concerning all the apparitions.

So even now, we cannot say everything about the message of

Fatima. And for many years one group or another will continue to emphasize this or that aspect of a message so varied, as each one views it from the perspective of personal need and personal devotion.

Lucia Explains

But Our Lady did not intend that we should be left guessing as to what the individual Catholic is expected to do in the wake of this "explosion of the supernatural". She said to Lucia: "You must remain here some time longer. Jesus wishes to make use of you to make me known..." And when Lucia felt these words like a "Sword piercing my heart" Our Lady added: "I will never leave you."

So in the midst of all the confusion, Lucia had been left in the world to speak to us. And in 1946, when the Bishop of Fatima invited two American writers to speak at length with Lucia, one of them spent his entire time... four consecutive hours... on only one question: "What does Our Lady WANT of us? What must the individual Catholic do in order that Communism may be turned back and the annihilation of nations averted?"

One of the reasons Lucia's answer took so many hours to reduce to simple statements is because the man interviewing her could hardly believe what she said. She spoke of an OFFERING of our daily duties, each day, and of living that offering.

But had Our Lady of Fatima said anything like this?

Lucia's "Formula"

She spoke of consecration to the Immaculate Heart of Mary, and of directing all our Marian devotion... especially the Rosary... towards sanctification of our daily duty. And the first Saturdays? She said they were important primarily as a means of purging oneself each month, of renewing one's purpose. The main requirement was the offering of sacrifices required by our state in life, using our devotion to Mary by consecration and Rosary, every day.

Towards the end of that four hour interview, with Lucia's help, a promise was formulated. It reads as follows:

"Dear Queen and Mother, who promised at Fatima to convert Russia and bring peace to all mankind, in reparation to your

Below, Pope Paul with the Rosary at feet of Our Lady of Fatima.

Immaculate Heart for my sins and the sins of the whole world, I solemnly promise: 1) To offer up every day the sacrifices demanded by my daily duty; 2) To say part of the Rosary daily while meditating on the Mysteries; 3) To wear the Scapular of Mt. Carmel as profession of this promise and as an act of consecration to you. I shall renew this promise often, especially in moments of temptation."

Bishop Approves

Fearful that he might have misunderstood, the American went back to see the Bishop of Fatima. He presented the brief promise with furrowed brow and asked anxiously: "Your Excellency, do you think this is indeed what people must do?" As the Bishop read the simple promise, his face brightened with almost every word. He handed back the promise and said:

"You may promulgate this as coming from me."

It was as though the Bishop himself had been longing to see the essential message of Fatima reduced to a simple, usable formula. From that time until his death he defended and promoted the formula throughout the world.

It happened that the American writer who received this formula from Lucia was editor of a magazine in the United States which had 160,000 subscribers. And immediately upon his return to America he began a campaign for signatures to the promise.

By the end of one year, over one and a quarter million American Catholics had signed the pledge.

Among them was a priest in Plainfield, N.J., who had attributed a cure of heart disease to Our Lady and made a vow to do all he could, for the rest of his life, to make her known. He preached the message of Fatima in his parish with great insistence.

One day, as he was about to begin his sermon, he wondered how many of those spread out before him in the church were actually doing what Our Lady asked, and he said:

"So that we may know who is fulfilling Our Lady's requests in this parish, let those who have made the promise wear something blue... and we, in this parish, will be Our Lady's Blue Army against the red tides of atheism."

From that day the idea of wearing something blue... and of calling those who signed the pledge the "Blue Army of Our Lady"... spread to neighboring parishes, to the entire United States, and finally to the world. It so pleased the Bishop of Fatima that he encouraged the building of a center at Fatima to promote fulfillment of the Fatima "pledge" under this title and his secretary once said: "It seems that His Excellency clings to life until the Blue Army is established in the world."

Clarified By Opposition

Opposition came to the pledge from many sides, particularly because of the morning offering and the scapular... which were not mentioned at Fatima.

Our Lady's first request of the children had been: "Do you wish to offer up to God all the sufferings He desires to send you in reparation for the sins by which He is offended, and in supplication for the conversion of sinners?" And the last thing Our Lady did, during the miracle of the sun itself, was to hold forth the Scapular.

But was this enough to choose these practices as a part of only four essential things to be done that the multiple requests of Our Lady of Fatima might be fulfilled?

Almost at once France asked permission of the Bishop of Fatima to substitute the miraculous medal for the scapular in the wording of the pledge.

The Bishop answered in the VOICE OF FATIMA, which was then published simultaneously in four languages, that the Blue Army had been correct in choosing the Scapular of Mount Carmel

"and no other" as the sign of consecration to the Immaculate Heart of Mary. And His Excellency referred to a recent statement of

Pope Pius XII to this effect. Lucia later said, when pressed on this point by V. Rev. Howard Rafferty, O. Carm.: "The scapular and the rosary are inseparable." And we can trust that final opposition was laid to rest by Pope Paul VI who, in his message to the first International Marian Congress after Vatican II said:

"You will make known our will and our exhortations which we base upon the dogmatic constitution of the Ecumenical Council Vatican II, which is in complete conformity with our thought and indeed upon which our thought is based:

Although the Blue Army began in 1947, it was not formally organized until 1950. In that year the Most Rev. Joseph Correia da Silva, Bishop of Fatima, sent the statue below as his personal gift to the U.S. Centre of the Blue Army with the prayer: "Through it may the Blessed Mother grant... to the Blue Army and to all those associated with it... a flood of graces and favors." During the ensuing years, the mantle of the statue changed to blue, although the tunic... with the same pigment... remained white. The Bishop's secretary said of the aged Bishop: "It seemed that he clung to life until the Blue Army was established in the world."

"'That one ever hold in great esteem the practices and exercises of the devotion to the most blessed Virgin which have been recommended for centuries by the Magisterium of the Church'. (#67) And among them we judge well to recall especially the Marian Rosary and the religious use of the Scapular of Mount Carmel...a form of piety which is adapted by its simplicity to the spirit indeed of everyone, and is most largely widespread among the faithful for an increase of spiritual fruit. *

"In these times when we instruct the Christian people, it is necessary constantly and clearly to inculcate the realization that insofar as the Mother is honored, so the Son...for Whom all exists (cf. Col. 1, 15-16)...will be known, loved, glorified as He should be, and that His commandments will be observed (#66, Constitution De Ecclesia, cited above); it is also necessary to advise the faithful that piety toward the Mother of God is not to be found in a sterile and passive sentimentalism nor in a certain vain credulity, but on the contrary that it proceeds by that true faith through which we are carried through a recognition of the eminence of the Mother of God, driven to a filial love toward our Mother and to the imitation of her virtues.'" (ibid, #67).

The Holy Father, in his letter to Cardinal Enriques to prepare His Eminence for the role of personal Legate of His Holiness at the Mariological Congress, continued:

"This then is what you will say, and that to which you will exhort the faithful using great care and solicitude to see that the holy solemnities over which you will preside in our name may be honored with total faith and a veneration full of devotion to the Holy Virgin Mary, Mother of God, Mother of the Church, Mother of Grace and of Mercy, Mother of Hope and of Holy Joy, she by whom we have access to Jesus and to the sources of salvation which are in Him, by a royal, direct way." *

Pledge Only First Step

Today, under the guidance of the present Bishop of Fatima and an International Council, the Blue Army of Our Lady promotes that simple pledge prepared with Lucia in 1946 as a "response to the message of Fatima".

It considers the pledge as an initial step, or the beginning of that life in Grace which the fulness of the message of Fatima promises. It does not pretend that the pledge contains ALL that Our Lady wishes of us.

As we look back at the past two decades of the Blue Army we can see the Hand of God in its origin, its development in the world, its sanction by the Bishop of Fatima and its approval by Rome. (The International Centre

---

*(Pius XII, Ep. Neminem profecto latet, 11 Feb. 1950; A. A. S. XLII, 390).

*(L'Osservatore Romano, April 2nd, 1965)

at Fatima was dedicated by Eugene Cardinal Tisserant not only in his own name, but as a legate of Pope Pius XII. And when the Cardinal returned to Fatima in 1967 with Pope Paul VI, he expressed regret that because of the brief time and vastness of the crowds he had not been able to proceed to the Blue Army House.)

But the greatest proof of the importance of the Blue Army pledge, which was prepared under Lucia's own guidance in 1946, is not so much in the many millions who have signed it but in its spiritual effect. And about this spiritual effect we have few statistics. Our time here would not permit enough specific examples to corroborate beyond doubt the wave of holiness that has been sweeping the world in the wake of the Blue Army of Our Lady.

Staggering Importance

It is difficult to believe that one little step like the Blue Army pledge... implemented by a morning offering and two very simple devotions... could make saints!

Yet this is what we have experienced, year after year, in nation after nation.

Out of the Blue Army has grown a movement of all-night vigils to the Blessed Sacrament which are now being made every month by thousands of lay persons all over the world! Out of the Blue Army has come a minor army of victim souls... who WELCOME suffering as a blessed way

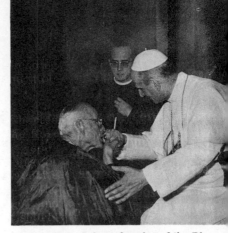

Above: Msgr. Colgan, founder of the Blue Army, greeting Pope Paul VI.

to obtain the conversion of more sinners!

As one who has been involved in this movement from the beginning I dare to say that nothing strikes me more out of the entire fact of Fatima, outside of the miracle of the sun itself, than the wave of holiness which follows in the wake of the fulfillment of this simple pledge. So much Grace from such a little practice!

Of course we are most easily aware of great manifestations of love and devotion like the all-night vigils. For example, in May of 1969, a Blue Army vigil was held for the first time in a church in New York... and the intention of each was to obtain the conversion of one thousand souls who would otherwise be lost. A priest who participated was so impressed with the atmosphere of holiness developed during the night that he exclaimed at the closing Mass: "I am convinced that you did obtain, in this night of love, one thousand souls for every person in this church."

And how many had come to this vigil, despite the fact that there was another vigil that same night in the same city and in neighboring cities?

There were almost five hundred lay persons there.

That would be five hundred thousand souls.

And what about the crusade among the sick? What about the hundreds of thousands who have made the pledge and whose lives are unknown to us?

Recently, a man was crushed in a fearful accident at Charleston, S. C. The lower part of his body was smashed, pelvis broken, bladder ruptured. For some inexplicable reason he never lost consciousness, and he never complained. As he was being taken to the hospital he merely asked if anyone could say the rosary with him. Later when an airline Captain said he had never seen such courage, the injured man said:

"All For Sinners"

"It is all for sinners. I am a member of the Blue Army."

This man joyfully accepted incredible suffering as though he personally had heard those words Our Lady first addressed to the children of Fatima: "Do you wish to offer up to God all the sufferings He desires to send you in reparation for the sins by which He is offended and in supplication for the conversion of sinners?"

What was the story of this injured man? Where had he obtained such heroic faith and devotion? Had he been a devout man all his life?

Here we come to the most amazing part of this example... and perhaps of the message of Fatima as it takes effect in the world:

This man had led a careless life. One day, in the back of a church, he saw a Blue Army pledge. He decided to make it.

That, and that alone, changed his life.

Within one year he not only gave up sin, but became a daily communicant. Then he began to say not just five decades of the Rosary a day, but fifteen. (How

Msgr. Colgan (extreme right) asks Father Pio (extreme left) to accept all Blue Army members as his "special children". John Haffert (facing Fr. Pio from doorway) heard Fr. Pio say: "Russia will be converted when there is a Blue Army member for every Communist."

many do this!) And then he began to long that he might obtain graces for others AS SOMEONE'S PRAYER HAD OBTAINED GRACE FOR HIM.

Can this be described as anything less than a wonder of Grace, from the Mother of all Graces? from the anxious Mother who came at Fatima not so much to frighten us with prophecies of events as to save us?

How Blue Army Works

Today, as twenty years ago, the Blue Army of Our Lady rests primarily on that simple pledge. The major goal of the Blue Army is to cause ALL Catholics to make that pledge and to live it.

Among the practical means of promoting the pledge are publications, such as SOUL in the United States, the VOICE in England and Australia, RALLY in Asia, SOL DE FATIMA in Spain, APPEL DE NOTRE DAME in France, CUORE DEL IMMACOLATA in Italy, and so on. Books and pamphlets are published in all major languages and distributed from centers in most countries around the world.

But personal contact is the most important means. And this is organized by Blue Army militants, governed by a set of rules approved "ad experimentum" by the Holy See in 1956. They are based on Canon Law and provide for a diocesan director and a priest counselor to any lay militants.

First Saturdays

Militants endeavor to have pamphlets and pledges available at the backs of churches, and to provide programs (such as the Pilgrim Virgin) explaining the message of Fatima in the various parishes. Above all, they promote the First Saturday devotion as a

In 1956, on the occasion of the dedication of the International Centre of the Blue Army at Fatima by His Eminence, Eugene Cardinal Tisserant, a set of rules to govern the Blue Army was approved for presentation to the Holy See. Officials at this meeting seen above, left to right, are: Most Rev. Joseph Correia da Silva, first Bishop of Fatima; Cardinal Tisserant; Bishop John Venancio, then Auxiliary Bishop of Fatima and now Bishop; and Monsignor Colgan, founder of the Blue Army, who conducted the meeting. Leaders of the movement from all parts of the world participated. The rules were adopted unanimously and have remained unchanged to the present time.

parish program, adopting the slogan: "First Saturday is Parish Day!"

Many who might not sign the pledge will at least promise to make the five First Saturdays... and before the five months are over, they are almost certain to sign the pledge. Sometimes the contrary is true. Some who would not make the five Saturdays, do agree to make the pledge. But then they follow by making the Five Saturdays, and they develop a spirit of penance, reparation, meditation, and devotion to the Blessed Sacrament.

The Ultimate Goal

The Blue Army sees the pledge and the First Saturdays not so much as goals to be achieved, but as means to the goal: Life in Grace. The pledge and the first Saturday devotions are their PRIMARY MEANS.

Today, at least in the United States, the Blue Army goes beyond the First Saturdays and the pledge in the CELL movement... which is an application of the message of Fatima in depth.

Two or three Blue Army members (this is the "cell") meet once a week for a meditated Rosary. They then discuss the spiritual ills of the day as manifest in events and in the public press. They encourage each other, as did the three children of Fatima, in the spirit of reparation. They practice the prayers taught to the children by Our Lady and the angels. And they try to become like

the children of Fatima: Victims for sinners.

When the "cell" grows to five or more members, it divides. That is how it grows. That is how it multiplies the holiness of Fatima in the Church. And that is why it is called a spiritual "cell".

Cardinal Tisserant called the Blue Army "The response to the requests of Our Lady of Fatima." That is what it was in the

beginning, and that is what it is now.

Anyone who recognizes the importance of Fatima must recognize the importance of APPLYING the message of Fatima in the world. And for that reason the Blue Army is of paramount importance.

In closing, we feel impelled to add one final thought although we find it very difficult to put into words.

The Battle Is Real

Never before in the records of history has God permitted a miracle at a predicted time and place "So that everyone may believe."

There is a battle being fought. It is worse than the battle exploding in Asia or lifting its bloodstained head out of the Sinai desert.

It is the battle between Satan and Our Lady.

International Centre of the Blue Army of Our Lady of Fatima taken from the Basilica.

You can serve in Catholic Charities, or even Propagation of the Faith. You can serve in the Sodality or even the Legion of Mary. And you may go for years in those apostolates without suffering contradiction, or public disgrace, or the apparent end to all your labors.

But not in the Blue Army.

Sometimes the blows against Blue Army militants and against the very name "Blue Army" seem mortal. It is as though a part of the body... in England, in America, even in Portugal as we once witnessed... is suddenly crushed to death.

Stronger Than Ever

And then... where the body seemed crushed to death... after a short time there is a stirring. Life is there! It is as though the humiliation and apparent defeat were sources of a new life. And suddenly the body there is not only alive, but stronger than ever!

For this reason, that American priest... Monsignor Harold Colgan... seems indeed (as he claims himself) to have spoken out of an inspiration from Our Lady when he gave to this apostolate the name "Army".

Only if we win the spiritual war (which Our Lady proclaimed to the death against Satan in 1917) shall we end the less important wars which so preoccupy the world.

I myself heard Father Pio, the famous stigmatic priest who died last year in the odor of sanctity, say:

"Russia will be converted when there is a Blue Army member for every Communist."

Over the vesting table in his sacristy, Father Pio had a statue of Our Lady of Fatima, and every day... as the spiritual father of all who KEEP the Blue Army pledge... he prayed for every member of the Blue Army. Lucia and the Carmelite Sisters of Coimbra do the same. So do cloistered sisters in many parts of the world. So do many, many dedicated souls.

And that is the fuel of this army: The fuel of holiness, derived from the Immaculate Heart of Mary for the triumph of the Sacred Heart of Jesus in all hearts in all the world.

When the Blue Army, with the Bishop of Fatima, took the Pilgrim Virgin to Czechoslovakia in October of 1967, Archbishop Tomasek of Prague said emotionally: "You have brought us the sign of our hope".

This is the mission of the Blue Army of Our Lady in all the world: To bring Our Lady's moral presence to all... to enable all to reach out and actually clasp the hands of their mother by means of the rosary and the scapular.

It is Our Lady Herself who does all the rest.